COOKIES ON THE LOWER SHELF™

Putting Bible Reading Within Reach

BY

PAM GILLASPIE

Cookies on the Lower Shelf

Copyright © 2012 by Pam Gillaspie
Published by Precept Ministries Interna-
tional
P.O. Box 182218
Chattanooga, Tennessee 37422
www.precept.org

ISBN 978-1-934884-83-6

COOKIES ON THE LOWER SHELF™

Putting Bible Reading Within Reach

Dedicated to . . .

Mom and Dad.

You taught me to love the stories and the God of the stories with my whole heart and I am forever grateful!

Acknowledgements

Thank you to my faithful friends who have studied with me over the years. We've learned that you can read or you can listen and that sometimes filling in all the blanks keeps you from wrestling with the real questions. I'm grateful for your patience in piloting this material and learning with me along the way.

Rick, Pete, Cress, and Dave—thank you for sludging through the editing, proofing, and design process with me. We all know that a book is never, ever a one-person job and I'm grateful to be part of a gifted team.

Brad and Katie—thank you for always putting up with me along the way!

TABLE OF CONTENTS

COOKIES ON THE LOWER SHELF™

Putting Bible Reading Within Reach

COOKIES ON THE LOWER SHELF™

Putting Bible Reading Within Reach

There is nothing quite like your favorite pair of jeans. You can dress them up, you can dress them down. You can work in them, play in them, shop in them . . . live in them. They always feel right. It is my hope that the structure of this Bible study will fit you like those jeans, that it will work with your life right now, right where you are whether you're new to this whole Bible thing or whether you've been studying the Book for years!

How is this even possible? Smoke and mirrors, perhaps? The beginner mercilessly thrown into the deep end of the exegetical? The experienced given pompoms and the job of simply cheering others on? None of the above.

Flexible Bible studies are designed with options that will allow you to go as deep each week as you desire. If you're just starting out and feeling a little overwhelmed, stick with the main text and don't think a second thought about the sidebar assignments. If you're looking for a challenge, then take the sidebar prompts and go ahead and dig all the way to China! As you move along through the study, think of the sidebars and "Digging Deeper" boxes as that 2% of lycra that you find in certain jeans . . . the wiggle-room that will help them fit just right.

Beginners may find that they want to start adding in some of the optional assignments as they go along. Experts may find that when three children are throwing up for three days straight, foregoing these assignments for the week is the way to live wisely.

Life has a way of ebbing and flowing and this study is designed to ebb and flow right along with it!

Enjoy!

How to use this study:

HOW TO USE THIS STUDY

Flexible inductive studies meet you where you are and take you as far as you want to go.

WEEKLY READING:

Main Reading
You'll find this text in the main column of the lesson. Read this—or listen to it—and you'll be able to follow the narrative and stay on track.

More Reading
These texts will give you more of the story. You'll typically find these located in the **One Step Further** boxes.

Even More Reading!
Finish these readings, too, and you'll read through the entire Bible by the time you finish the *Cookies* series. These readings are often in the **Digging Deeper** boxes.

1. **WEEKLY STUDY:** The main text guides you through the complete topic of study for the week.

2. **FYI boxes:** For Your Information boxes provide bite-sized material to shed additional light on the topic.

> **FYI:**
>
> **Reading Tip: Begin with prayer**
> You may have heard this a million times over and if this is a million and one, so be it. Whenever you read or study God's Word, first pray and ask His Spirit to be your Guide.

3. **ONE STEP FURTHER and other sidebar boxes:** Sidebar boxes give you the option to push yourself a little further. If you have extra time or are looking for an extra challenge, you can try one, all, or any number in between! These boxes give you the ultimate in flexibility.

> **ONE STEP FURTHER:**
>
> **Word Study: *torah*/law**
> The first of eight Hebrew key words we encounter for God's Word is *torah*, translated "law." If you're up for a challenge this week, do a word study to learn what you can about *torah*. Run a concordance search and examine where the word *torah* appears in the Old Testament and see what you can learn from the contexts.
>
> If you decide to look for the word for "law" in the New Testament, you'll find that the primary Greek word is *nomos*.
>
> Be sure to see what Paul says about the law in Galatians 3 and what Jesus says in Matthew 5.

4. **DIGGING DEEPER boxes:** If you're looking to go further, Digging Deeper sections will help you sharpen your skills as you continue to mine the truths of Scripture for yourself.

> ## Digging Deeper
>
> **What else does God's Word say about counselors?**
>
> If you can, spend some time this week digging around for what God's Word says about counselors.
>
> Start by considering what you already know about counsel from the Word of God and see if you can actually show where these truths are in the Bible. Make sure that the Word actually says what you think it says.

Week One
Beginnings

"For this commandment which I command you today is not too difficult for you, nor is it out of reach . . . But the word is very near you, in your mouth and in your heart, that you may observe it."
—Deuteronomy 30:11,14

God's Word was not meant to be held behind locked doors. It was not delivered to man only to be hoarded, grudgingly dispensed, or rationed by the elite to the masses. God's Words are light and life! Parents are to teach them in the morning, speak of them along the path, discuss them over lunch, and consider them at bedtime. God designed His Word to be part of the fabric of our lives, moving with us, instructing our thoughts and behaviors. Just listen to the words of God in Deuteronomy 6:4-9:

"Hear, O Israel! The LORD is our God, the LORD is one! You shall love the LORD your God with all your heart and with all your soul and with all your might. These words, which I am commanding you today, shall be on your heart. You shall teach them diligently to your sons and shall talk of them when you sit in your house and when you walk by the way and when you lie down and when you rise up. You shall bind them as a sign on your hand and they shall be as frontals on your forehead. You shall write them on the doorposts of your house and on your gates."

God's words were meant for common people—people just like you and me. God spoke accessible and understandable words to the fathers by the prophets and then He came nearer still when He spoke in His Son. God's Word was meant to be near people, to be understood, consumed and lived, but man's fallen history of exchanging truth for lies has included confounding the clear and removing the near. Man decided to be consumed by other things—created things. These became his life.

This study is all about showing how these sweet words are accessible cookies on the lower shelf.

THIS WEEK:

Main Reading
8.5 chapters
- Genesis 1-4: Creation
- Genesis 6-9: Noah
- Genesis 11:1-9: Tower of Babel

Additional Reading

More Reading
10 chapters
- Genesis 5: Genealogy
- Genesis 10: Genealogy
- Job 1-3; 38-42

Even More Reading!
36 chapters
- Complete book of Job

COOKIES ON THE LOWER SHELF™
Putting Bible Reading Within Reach

CONSIDER the WAY you THINK

What successes or failures have you had in reading the Bible?

What characterizes your reading and/or studying?

Have you encountered any hang-ups along the way? If so, what kinds?

What has worked for you?

Are you bringing any fears or reservations to this study? If so, what are they?

What do you hope to gain through this study?

Putting Bible Reading Within Reach

Notes

READING THE STORY
OBSERVE the TEXT of SCRIPTURE

READ the account of Creation in Genesis 1–4 and briefly summarize below.

RECORD key words and phrases you noticed.

DISCUSS with your GROUP or PONDER on your own . . .

How does the Bible start?

Who is the main character in the first two chapters? What did He do?

Describe God's creation briefly. What characterized it? Was it flawed in any way? Explain.

What did God create on the sixth day? What instructions did God give?

FYI:

Key Words

Key words unlock the meanings of texts. **They're** often repeated and are critical to understanding messages. As you read, watch for **important words and phrases that repeat.** If you mark **key words** along with **their** pronouns and synonyms, you'll be able to identify **them** much more quickly on the page.

ONE STEP FURTHER:

Genesis 1:1, John 1:1 and John 1:14

According to John 1:1 and 1:14, who else was involved at creation? How do the opening verses of Genesis and John compare? Record your observations below.

COOKIES ON THE **LOWER SHELF**™
Putting Bible Reading Within Reach

5

What did God do on the seventh day?

ONE STEP FURTHER:

Genesis 5: The Genealogy from Adam

If you've been knocked out of Bible reading in Genesis, chances are it was at Genesis 5, 10, 11, or 36. Why? Genealogies. Seriously, there's nothing like a list of names in the middle of a narrative to make you feel like doing something else. While genealogies aren't usually compelling reading, we can learn a lot by studying them.

If you're up for paying a little extra attention today, work your way through Genesis 5 and record your observations below. If it still sounds like a bad idea, try reading the genealogy another time. Remember, part of learning to enjoy this study will involve allowing the homework to flex to meet you.

What did God tell Adam and Eve to do? Did they have a lot of commands? Look closely and record what God told them to do and not to do.

How did the serpent deceive Eve? Look closely at the sequence.

What steps preceded Eve's sin? What did she do before she ate? Do you see places in the narrative where she could have changed her mind and stopped short of eating?

How did Adam respond when God confronted him?

What can we learn about temptation and deception from the pattern the serpent and Eve modeled?

Digging Deeper

Is Sabbath still for me?

Spend some time this week examining the concept of sabbath in the Bible and investigating how you can apply it today.

Where is sabbath first mentioned?

What is the context?

Where else do we see it in the Old Testament? In the New Testament?

FYI:

Don't Break Up the Story
Here's the deal. This is a flexible study and in flexing you're not bound to a specific amount of reading. I have one strong suggestion, though. As you work through the material during the week, try not to break up stories. In other words, read the creation account all the way through. You may need to review and answer the questions later but try to read an account in one sitting. I understand some of your life situations will make this difficult. If you can't do it like this, just do it whatever way you can. If you can, however, you'll do well to learn to read the Bible account by account and book by book. This is very different from the way we often go about it—reading three chapters a day or snippets here and there. At least give it a shot. Context is crucial and reading larger segments in single sittings helps us pay attention to context and increase attention span.

Did Jesus honor sabbaths? Explain.

What application can you make in your life?

Is the sabbath still valid? Why/why not?

How can you incorporate sabbath principles into your life?

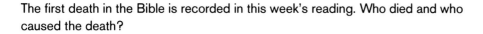

The first death in the Bible is recorded in this week's reading. Who died and who caused the death?

What promise did God make in the aftermath of Adam and Eve's sin? (Genesis 3:15)

OBSERVE the TEXT of SCRIPTURE

READ the account of Noah in Genesis 6–9 and briefly summarize below.

RECORD key words and phrases you noticed.

DISCUSS with your GROUP or PONDER on your own . . .

What characterized the moral climate between the time of Adam and Noah? During Noah's lifetime, how did God view the state of mankind?

Describe Noah. How did he differ from the rest of the people?

FYI:

How long will it take?
Listening to Genesis 1–10 on *The Bible Experience* MP3 will take you under 45 minutes. Pass over the genealogies and your run time will be less!

COOKIES ON THE LOWER SHELF™
Putting Bible Reading Within Reach

Before Noah's time, what did people eat? How did this change after the flood?

How did man's relationship with animals change after the flood?

Describe the covenant God made. Who did He make it with? (Be careful; it's not just Noah!)

OBSERVE the TEXT of SCRIPTURE

READ the account of The Tower of Babel in Genesis 11:1-9 and briefly summarize below.

RECORD key words and phrases you noticed.

DISCUSS with your GROUP or PONDER on your own . . .

What command did God give to Adam and Eve and to Noah's family?

What were the people doing at Babel? What did this reveal about their hearts?

How did God intervene? What happened?

Do you ever find yourself caught up in something that seems great and noble but is counter to God? If so, how do you identify it?

Digging Deeper

The first book written? Seriously?

People who pick up a chronological Bible are often surprised to find the book of Job staring at them for the first few days of their reading. While Job appears in about the middle of the traditional Christian Bible, scholars believe it was probably the first book recorded. Although it's a little difficult to read, it's an account of redemption from tragic suffering that fits the Bible's overall theme of redemption—God's plan to save His people through and out of tribulation.

Who was Job? How did God describe him?

What sufferings did Job endure? How did he respond to them?

ONE STEP FURTHER:

Genesis 11: The Genealogy of Shem

Yes, it's another genealogy. Noah's sons Ham, Shem, and Japheth are the super-great-grandfathers of everyone today. In the closing verses of Genesis 11 we read about Shem's descendants. Who are they and why are they important? Record your findings below.

How did his friends respond? How about his wife?

What did you learn about God from the book of Job?

What did you learn from Job's life that you can apply in yours?

@THE END OF THE DAY . . .

What has been your biggest takeaway this week?

Do you need to make any priority adjustments in your life to make more room for God and His Word? If so, what?

Spend some time with God quietly reflecting on what you have learned. Record your thoughts below.

FYI:

A Word from a Recovering Type A

Just a gentle reminder to let this study flex! I know I've already laid out the "flex facts" but this is the exhortation to take it to heart. Think this through with me. If a study actually flexes to meet both new students and highly advanced students, reality says that most students will not finish all the homework every week. Type A personalities I'm talking to you! Learn to relax with this material. Relish the text of Scripture and find a pace that brings joy! Some weeks you may read the text of Scripture and never pick up a pencil for the workbook while other weeks you may be adding pages to the workbook for all your notes. Some weeks you may read the Bible; other weeks you can choose to listen to it. Let it flex.

If you've just had a serious "Type A reaction" (remember, it takes one to know one!) I have one additional assignment for you: Pick at least one sidebar or **Digging Deeper** section NOT to complete this coming week. Counterintuitive? Probably, but sometimes growth in grace hurts in strange ways.

WEEK TWO
Blessings for a Flawed Follower

*By faith Abraham, when he was tested, offered up Isaac,
and he who had received the promises was offering up his
only begotten son . . .*
—Hebrews 11:17

While it might sound odd, one of the reasons I am such a big Old Testament fan is because in it I see God stooping down and redeeming flawed people time after time after time. It's not an account filled with mostly good people and an occasional problem child. No, the Old Testament is packed with murderers, adulterers, doubters, and others who threatened to wear down even the most resolute to a nub. People also dealt with everything from relocation and recession to infertility and blended families. Some had it all; others lost all. If we can get past our presuppositions and familiarity with the stories, we'll see people dealing with the same things we face today. You think blended families are hard today? Think about blending two (or more!) wives with one husband! And if infertility is hard today, imagine dealing with it when the only treatment option was another wife. Yes, our lives are complicated, but in many ways this text takes "complicated" to entirely new levels!

And while our lives are hard, the verse at the top of this page also takes "hard" to a whole new level.

*Note: Hebrews will be a main text reading in *Cookies on the Lower Shelf, Part III* and will appear in a **Digging Deeper** assignment on Leviticus in a couple of weeks. If you don't have time this week, save it for later. Hebrews provides compelling commentary on a number of Old Testament books, so you'll see it resurface more than once.

COOKIES ON THE LOWER SHELF™
Putting Bible Reading Within Reach

Notes

Following the Story . . .

This week's reading follows the life and times of Abraham. You'll notice that he's born with the name Abram but God changes it along the way. If you can carve out the time, I highly suggest you read the material in one sitting or two tops and then work through the questions referring back to the text as you go. I'm suggesting this approach because the text this week covers Abraham's whole life. I want you to interact with this as a single history, as you would a biography, as opposed to a series of disjointed magazine articles. Make sense? If time doesn't allow then go ahead and read smaller portions but consider this your opportunity to justify a mocha and a morning at your local coffee shop. More than anything this way of doing the assignment is about shifting your paradigm from reading nibbles to reading chunks and this is a perfect text for the job. This week's reading will overlap a bit with next week's so we can read the entire Abraham account. So don't be concerned when the reading goes to Genesis 25 while the questions stop at Genesis 22!

REMEMBERING

Before you start reading take a couple of minutes and summarize the story from last week. This is an exercise in both recall and brevity! Keep it short and simple. Look back if you need to.

READING THE STORY
ABRAHAM at 75–86 YEARS OLD

OBSERVE the TEXT of SCRIPTURE
READ the account of Abram's early years in Genesis 11:26–Genesis 14 and briefly summarize below.

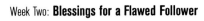

COOKIES ON THE LOWER SHELF™
Putting Bible Reading Within Reach

FYI:

Defining Terms: True Story

A key inductive Bible study skill is paying attention to context. It's hard to understand words—or anything else for that matter—apart from surroundings.

Often today the word "story" sits in a context of fictional tales, myths, or half-truths. The setting colors the meaning of the word.

The setting of "story" in the context of Bible study also colors the meaning of the word. In the context of this book, the assumption is that we are talking about absolute truth.

Notes

RECORD key words and phrases you noticed.

DISCUSS with your GROUP or PONDER on your own . . .

At the beginning of Genesis 12, what did God call Abram to do?

What did He promise Abram? (Watch for two distinct aspects to the promise.)

How did Abram respond?

How old was Abram?

Has God ever called you to a path you couldn't see the end of? How did you respond? Why? What can you learn in situations like this from the account of Abram?

FYI:

Don't forget to pray!
Remember to pray as you read. The Holy Spirit guides us into all truth. Praying invites Him to do this and reminds us that what we learn is dependent on His revealing truth to us.

FYI:

So what's the Negev?
Every now and then, biblical translators leave us hanging with a word like *Negev*, as in "Abraham journeyed on, continuing toward the Negev." *Negev* is Hebrew for *south*. So how to remember this? Tell the kids or grandkids that you're going to the *Negev* to see Mickey Mouse and I'll bet they'll help you remember it!

COOKIES ON THE
LOWER SHELF™
Putting Bible Reading Within Reach

17

Notes

Where did Abram and his clan end up settling? What event in Genesis 12:10 caused them to leave for a time? Where did they go?

FYI:

It's About the Word

Just a quick reminder that the goal of this study is to get you into God's Word for yourself. The questions in this workbook are designed to help you think through the text and provide some loose structure. If you ever have a week where it comes down to a choice between reading more text or writing more answers, it's my prayer that you will always opt for God's Words over man's questions—in this or any other study. Bible study materials are not the end; they are means to help you get into the Word for yourself!

What questionable behavior did Abram exhibit in the latter part of Genesis 12? How did he rationalize it?

Was Abram thinking clearly when he did this? Why/why not? Reason from the text of Scripture taking into account God's promise to him.

ONE STEP FURTHER:

Watch for the Repeats

Throughout Genesis keep your eyes peeled for sins that repeat from generation to generation. If you watch closely you'll see favoritism, deception, and other recurring evils, often within families. As you see examples, take note. If you know of any off the top of your head, start your list. Record your observations below.

Are you ever tempted to "bend the truth" in potentially dangerous situations? What can you do to stop this?

Why did Abram and Lot separate in Genesis 13?

Digging Deeper

Keeping the Word in the Front of the Mind

Memorizing has a bad rep in certain circles. Some associate it with school and forced learning; others think they're flat-out too old. But memorizing remains a powerful tool for followers of Jesus Christ because it keeps God's Word in front of them throughout the day.

Since the first two parts of the *Cookies* material will focus primarily on the Old Testament, I want to suggest a New Testament memorization project for you to consider. Sit down. I'm going to throw the whole steak on the plate so you can decide how much you'd like to have.

This week I'd like you to read through the Sermon on the Mount in Matthew 5–7 and consider memorizing all or part of it over the time period for this class. If you stick with it for all three parts, that averages out to one chapter per class!

I know, some of you think I'm crazy. I can live with that. Like I said, read through the material and see if there is something in there that God leads you to commit to memory.

Worriers might want to recall Matthew 6:24-34, for example.

Think about it and pray about it this week. If God lays a verse or portion of the passage on your heart, record it below and let someone know that you're going to do it. Telling someone will help your resolve.

ONE STEP FURTHER:

Mark the Promises
As you read the Abraham account mark every reference you see to *descendants* and *land*. These are God's two big promises to Abraham, which have continuing significance even today!

FYI:

Do I have to mark texts?
Of course not! There is nothing magical about **marking** texts. What it does, though, is make important words and concepts stand out on the page. Do you have to **mark**? No. Does it help? Yes.

If **marking** texts is going to put you in a bad frame of mind, don't do it. But if you can keep an open mind, give **marking** it a try! You may be surprised how helpful **marking** can be in making key words jump off the page.

I'll bet you weren't looking for a key word in this sidebar. I'll also bet that you can tell me what the key word is!

COOKIES ON THE LOWER SHELF™
Putting Bible Reading Within Reach

Which part of the land did Lot choose? Briefly describe it.

Describe the people of Sodom and Gomorrah.

Genesis 14 recounts an ancient war between several kings. Without getting bogged down, briefly summarize how Lot first got involved and then Abraham.

Describe Melchizedek. Who was he and what did he do? (Answer from the text.)

How did Abram respond to Melchizedek?

Where can we find additional information on Melchizedek? If you're not sure, what resources can you explore?

Digging Deeper

Who is Melchizedek?

If you have extra time this week look more closely at the shadowy figure named Melchizedek who crashes onto the scene at the end Genesis 14 and exits just as abruptly.

Where else is Melchizedek mentioned in the Bible? What do the cross-references tell us?

Are there other examples of pre-Levitical priests in the Bible? Explain.

How is Jesus compared to Melchizedek?

What argument does the author of Hebrews make regarding Melchizedek?

Based on your study, what do you make of Melchizedek?

Finally, how do your commentaries weigh in on the person of Melchizedek? Do you agree? Disagree? Why?

FYI:

The "When" of Commentary Use
Bible commentaries can be very helpful in the study process but only after you've done your own homework! You pray. You read. You study. You think. You check a concordance and cross-references and *then* you consult them.

COOKIES ON THE **LOWER SHELF**™
Putting Bible Reading Within Reach

Notes

OBSERVE the TEXT of SCRIPTURE

READ Genesis 15–16 and briefly summarize below.

RECORD any key words and phrases you noticed.

ONE STEP FURTHER:

Memory opportunity!
After this, the word of the LORD came to Abram in a vision: "Do not be afraid, Abram. I am your shield, your very great reward."
–Genesis 15:1 (NIV)

ONE STEP FURTHER:

Romans on Abraham's Faith
Take a little time this week to see what Paul says in Romans 4 about Abraham's faith and how it relates to righteousness. Record your findings below.

DISCUSS with your GROUP or PONDER on your own . . .

What did God tell Abram after he met with Melchizedek? How did He make His promise to Abram more specific?

How did Abram respond?

What did God tell Abram about his descendants? What future event awaited them? How long would it last?

Genesis 16:3 tells us Abram and Sarai had lived in the land of Canaan for ten years. What still hadn't happened? How old were they at this point?

After ten years of waiting for a child, what did Sarai do?

Although this may strike your last nerve, how did Sarai explain her action? Do we see similar incidents elsewhere in Scripture? If so, where?

Did Sarai achieve her desired result? Explain.

Have you ever doubted God like Sarai? What did God teach you?

What other parties were affected by Sarah's action and how?

Think carefully before you answer this: Did Sarai's plan appear to work? Why? Why not?

COOKIES ON THE LOWER SHELF™

Putting Bible Reading Within Reach

23

ABRAHAM at 99 YEARS OLD AND BEYOND

OBSERVE the TEXT of SCRIPTURE

READ Genesis 17–25 and briefly summarize below.

RECORD any key words and phrases you noticed.

Digging Deeper

Soaking in the Book of Hebrews

If you're craving some New Testament reading or simply have some extra time week, read through the book of Hebrews. You'll learn more about Melchizedek and get a primer on Moses and the sacrificial system before we head into the books of Exodus, Leviticus, and Numbers.

Record your observations below. Do note that this is not the last opportunity you'll have to read the complete book of Hebrews in this study!

DISCUSS with your GROUP or PONDER on your own . . .

How old was Abraham when God appeared to him according to Genesis 17?

What promise did God repeat?

What additional details did God give Abraham about the seed?

What sign did God give in the chapter? Why?

How did Abraham react to God's promise of a son through his wife? Did this surprise you? Why/why not?

Who delivered news to Abraham in Genesis 18? What news did he bring?

COOKIES ON THE LOWER SHELF™
Putting Bible Reading Within Reach

Week Two: **Blessings for a Flawed Follower**

How did Sarah react to the news?

While Abraham and Sarah were getting good news, what was going on in Sodom and Gomorrah?

Do you recall who lived in Sodom?

How does this explain the concern Abraham had for the city?

How did God meet Abraham at his place of concern?

What happened in Genesis 19 when the angels arrived in Sodom?

How did the people of the city act toward them?

FYI:

Moab and Ammon

The opening chapters of Genesis give us loads of background information on people and nations who show up later in the biblical story. By paying attention early on we can save ourselves hours of head-scratching later. I'll be pulling some of the most significant connections out in sidebars like this one.

A concordance search on *Moab/Moabite* yields 203 hits in 178 verses; *Ammon/ Ammonites* returns 127 hits in 119 verses. These are major players who interact throughout the Old Testament times with the people of Israel. Often we're tempted to gloss over names like *Moab* and *Ammon* without a second thought and lump them in the pile of "nations around Israel." What's interesting and significant, though, is that many of the nations around Israel have some common roots with her. In Genesis we're given the disturbing yet memorable account of the beginning of the nations of Moab and Ammon.

The men who would become the fathers of the nations of Moab and Ammon were both the sons of Lot, one by each of his daughters. The part to remember here is that Moab and Ammon are not just unrelated pagan nations. They are related to each other and both are related to Abram and his descendants. If you can keep track of how the surrounding nations are related to Israel, you will be well on your way to understanding the people groups and, believe it or not, the geography of the Bible. We'll get to that point in a little bit!

COOKIES ON THE LOWER SHELF™

Putting Bible Reading Within Reach

Notes

What eventually happened to the city? To Lot and his family?

What two cities were destroyed? What two nations were birthed?

According to Genesis 20, as Abraham and Sarah headed for Gerar, what deception do we see repeated?

What happened to Sarah as a result?

What did God tell Abimelech in the dream?

Abram's prayer for Abimelech—the first occurrence of pray (palal) in the Bible—is right here when Abram is told to pray for Abimelech. In response God healed Abimelech and his wife and maids and they bore children. Guess who bears a child in the next chapter? That's right—Sarah. As you read about Isaac and his wife facing infertility, watch closely how he handles the situation!

FYI:

Easing into the Geography of Israel

I know. You didn't sign up for a geography class. I get that. I never cared much for geography either but I'm finally starting to get the hang of biblical geography and appreciating how helpful knowing it is.

So here's your first ease-into-it fact: The nation of Israel is only about the size of New Jersey, roughly 1,300 square miles less than the state of Massachusetts. Those states, my friend, are tiny!

Add to this the fact that Israel is bordered along its entire western edge by the Mediterranean Sea and you have a simple place to start. That's all for now. It's small and one edge is just water! Simple, right?

COOKIES ON THE LOWER SHELF™

Putting Bible Reading Within Reach

Week Two: **Blessings for a Flawed Follower**

How old was Abraham when Isaac was born?

What happened to Ishmael as Isaac grew and was weaned?

What did God promise to do for Ishmael?

Genesis 22 contains a disturbing account, at least on the surface. It's the kind of story that makes kids fall asleep with one eye open. As you read and answer the questions, keep in mind what Abraham knew and when he knew it.

What did God ask Abraham to do?

How did Abraham respond?

When Abraham took Isaac to the mountain, what did he tell the young men?

Digging Deeper

How well do you know your God?

The author of Hebrews tells us that Abraham "considered [*logisamenos:* having reasoned] that God was able even to raise [Isaac] from the dead." Abraham acted in faith because he knew God. Take some time today to go for a walk or sit quietly and consider how well you know your God. Ask Him how you can know Him better. As you consider this question, also think about specific situations where you would live differently if you knew God better and trusted Him more. Record your thoughts below.

What facts did Abraham know by this time?
  –What did he know about God?

  –What did he know about the promise?

  –What did he know about who the promise would come through?

What does Hebrews 11:17-19 tell us about what Abraham knew and "considered"?

Does this commentary in Hebrews affect your view of the events? If so, how?

@THE END OF THE DAY . . .

I hope you're starting to feel the flow of the narrative. Reading the Bible takes effort but I'm confident you'll find your work worthwhile! Next week the pace will pick up a little bit but remember you have alternate ways to get in the Word and get it in you. Use an iPod, let your computer read to you, read to your kids or grandkids. Be creative. As we close, spend some quiet time reflecting on and writing down the most important lesson you learned from Abraham's life. How can you begin applying it this week?

WEEK THREE

Same Promise, More Problems

Then Esau said, "Let us take our journey and go, and I will go before you." But [Jacob] said to him, "My lord knows that the children are frail and that the flocks and herds which are nursing are a care to me. And if they are driven hard one day, all the flocks will die."
—Genesis 33:12-13

He tends his flock like a shepherd: He gathers the lambs in his arms and carries them close to his heart; he gently leads those that have young.
—Isaiah 40:11 (NIV)

How are you doing in reading or listening to the Word? While it may seem like we're overstaying our welcome in Genesis, the reason for our lengthy sojourn is two-fold. First, Genesis is crammed full of foundational material. While we can skim over a genealogy here or there, for the most part this book is a *Who's Who* guide to everything that follows. In Genesis we find out who is related to whom and how they ended up where they're at. Some of it may rush past us, but like an early episode of a spell-binding drama we pick up continual hints and reminders of who belongs where and why. Will you remember it *all* the first time? Of course not. Still, you'll likely retain enough to retrace your steps and find answers you need.

The second reason we're taking an extended stay here is this: I don't want to lose anyone. In future weeks, it will be easier to increase the bonus reading and keep it in step with the main reading but in Genesis almost all of the text is critical-to-the-main-story material. If we speed it up now we may do so at the expense of people who desperately need to know the history. In bringing people to the Word of God, there's no such thing as acceptable losses.

So if you're looking for more this week, you'll have the opportunity to hang out with Jesus in Matthew or to simply linger in the times of Isaac and Jacob, slowing down long enough to see their experiences more closely and learn from their successes and failures.

THIS WEEK:

Main Reading
10 chapters
- Genesis 26: Isaac
- Genesis 27-35: Jacob

Additional Reading

More Reading
3 chapters
- Genesis 24-25: Reread Isaac context
- Genesis 36: Esau genealogy

Even More Reading!
28 chapters
- Complete book of Matthew

Note: This is not your last chance to read Matthew! We'll cover it again in *Cookies on the Lower Shelf, Part III.* This is a bonus reading for those who need more than 10 chapters to keep them going this week.

COOKIES ON THE LOWER SHELF™

Putting Bible Reading Within Reach

Week Three: **Same Promise, More Problems**

Following the Story . . .

We began with God in the beginning. We watched Him create the world and then Adam and Eve, then we watched man fall into sin. Cain killed Abel and Seth was born. Enoch walked with God while the world plunged deeper into sin. God sent a flood to destroy everything in the world except righteous Noah, his family, two of each kind of animal, and seven of every clean animal.

REMEMBERING

Before you start reading this week, take a couple of minutes to summarize last week's events. Remember, we're going for short, simple, and memorable. Check your notes or Bible only if you need to.

READING THE STORY

ISAAC and the final years of ABRAHAM

OBSERVE the TEXT of SCRIPTURE

READ the account of Isaac's life and briefly summarize below. Depending on the time you have available, you can do this in one of two ways.

> **SHORT OPTION:** Pick up where we left off last week and read Genesis 26. Although the Isaac material doesn't end until Genesis 28, Jacob becomes the main character in Genesis 27–35.

> **LONGER OPTION:** Backtrack and pick up more of the context of Isaac's adult life starting with Genesis 24 and reading through Genesis 26.

RECORD a brief summary of Isaac's life.

RECORD key words and phrases you noticed.

DISCUSS with your GROUP or PONDER on your own . . .
FINDING A WIFE FOR ISAAC

How did Abraham find a wife for Isaac? What factors made this difficult?

How did Abraham's faith increase over the years? Compare what he did here and earlier.

Where did the servant go on his mission?

Okay, you got the "book answer." Now, can you locate it on a map? Explain.

How did the servant approach his task?

What happened?

ONE STEP FURTHER:

Word Study: Successful
If you have some extra time this week, examine the word translated *successful (tsalach)* in Genesis 24:40. Find where else it's used in this chapter and in the Old Testament. Record what you learn below.

Digging Deeper

Leveraging Monster Chapters: Genesis 25

Every word of the Bible is inspired, literally God-breathed. Every book, chapter, verse, and word is important. Certain sections of the Word, though, pack extra punch. You can't deny John 3:16, Romans 4:5, and all of Romans 8 are theologically packed. Genesis 25, likewise, is historically and contextually dense. It shows up smack dab in the middle of the book of Genesis and gives us a one-chapter snapshot of the patriarchs and their significant others. If you have some extra time this week hang out in this powerhouse chapter and make yourself a family tree with explanations of who everyone is and how they relate to one another. Then draw a simple map to locate the areas associated with specific people.

FAMILY TREE

MAP

Notes

COOKIES ON THE LOWER SHELF™

Putting Bible Reading Within Reach

What was Abraham's family life like after Sarah died? Why is this significant?

What does the text tell us about Abraham's death?

ISAAC AFTER THE DEATH SARAH

How old was Isaac when he married?

What problem did Isaac and Rebekah have in common with Abraham and Sarah?

How long did it persist? How long did it persist for Isaac's parents?

What did Isaac do for his wife? Compare this with his parents' actions.

What principles can you take from Isaac's life and apply to your own?

FYI:

Placing Aram and Egypt

We've already conceded that geography is not the most scintillating topic ever. Still it can be interesting, helpful, and nearly painless if you learn it one or two pieces at a time.

That said, I'm going to throw two pieces at you right now but only because you can remember them together as opposite points on a compass both geographically and relationally. Here they are:

Aram is NORTHEAST of Israel ("Canaan" in the days of the patriarchs). It is the homeland of Laban, Rebekah, Rachel, and Leah. It is the country of Abraham's relatives where Jacob spent about 20 years earning his women and flock. When Isaac needed a wife, Abraham sent his servant to Aram to find one because the land of Canaan (although it would later become Israel) was still a land of foreigners. Aram, in the book of Genesis, is a FAMILY place.

Egypt is SOUTHWEST of Israel (Canaan). It is the land Abraham traveled to in search of food during a famine. As we'll see next week, it is also the land Abraham's great-grandson Joseph ruled as "vice president." Eventually it became the land of a 400-year Hebrew enslavement. Along with Canaan, Egypt is a FOREIGN place. If we want to run with the "**f**" motif, it is the **f**oreign land people **f**led to during **f**amines.

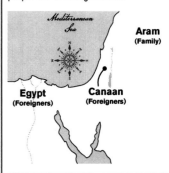

Describe the family dynamics in Isaac and Rebekah's house.

ONE STEP FURTHER:

More relatives: Midian

Among Abraham's sons by Keturah, none stands out more than Midian. If you have extra time this week, run a concordance search on *Midian* and see what you can find out about this "other son" of Abraham. Record your findings below.

How did both parents' favoritism affect family life? (Remember this, as it will be a recurring family pattern.) What lessons can we learn from their behavior?

How did Jacob, the second born, end up with his brother's birthright?

Genesis 26 revolves solely around Isaac. In it we see a sin he picked up from his father, but we also see the Abrahamic covenant being renewed with him.

What negative example did Isaac follow? How did it turn out for him?

What happened when God appeared to Isaac? What did He say to him? How does it compare with God's words to Abraham?

What were Esau's wives like?

COOKIES ON THE **LOWER SHELF**™

Putting Bible Reading Within Reach

READING THE STORY

JACOB: DECEPTION and FLIGHT

OBSERVE the TEXT of SCRIPTURE

READ Genesis 27–28 and briefly summarize below.

RECORD key words and phrases you noticed.

DISCUSS with your GROUP or PONDER on your own . . .

How did second-born Jacob end up with the blessing?

Who hatched and directed the plot?

How did Jacob react? What was "right" about his behavior? What was wrong?

What family problems do you see being lived out? Are these common to problems families have today? Explain.

Notes

When the deed was done, how did Esau react?

What consequences did Jacob and Rebekah reap?

What happened to Jacob on his way to Uncle Laban's?

What did Jacob name the place and why?

How did Jacob respond? What did he vow?

READING THE STORY

JACOB: LIFE IN ARAM and the RETURN HOME

OBSERVE the TEXT of SCRIPTURE

READ Genesis 29–35 and briefly summarize below.

RECORD key words and phrases you noticed.

DISCUSS with your GROUP or PONDER on your own . . .

What happened when Jacob arrived in Uncle Laban's neighborhood?

Who did Jacob love?

What agreement did Jacob and Laban make?

What happened at the end of the seven years?

Do you see any irony in the situation? What family trait showed itself?

Do you have any less-than-admirable family traits in your tree? If so, what? What action will you take to see that these aren't passed down to future generations?

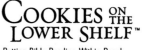

What did Rachel have in common with Sarah and Rebekah? How did each deal with the problem they faced?

FYI:

The trickster gets tricked!
Don't miss the irony of the trickster being tricked. Jacob works seven years for Rachel and ends up with her older sister Leah. After completing the marriage week with Leah, Uncle Laban gives him Rachel on credit but he then has to work another seven years to "pay her off." Deception runs strong in this family. Mamma Rebekah and Jacob tricked Isaac out of a blessing and now Rebekah's brother tricks Jacob into an extra wife.

Who bore Jacob's children?

What children were born to which mothers?

Why was this group of sons so significant? What nation do they eventually become?

THE RETURN HOME

Why did Jacob decide to leave Laban?

How did Jacob's wives respond to his plan? Why?

Describe Jacob's departure. What characterized it?

How long had Jacob been with Laban?

Who was supposed to call him back home? When? Did this ever happen?

Who did call Jacob back?

What parties made a covenant and why?

What was Jacob's emotional condition in this chapter? Explain.

What did Jacob do with his emotions? What can we learn from his behavior?

What was his plan for dealing with Esau?

Notes

Week Three: **Same Promise, More Problems**

What happened to Jacob the night before he met Esau?

ONE STEP FURTHER:

How old were they?

I was raised with Bible stories at bedtime and I'm grateful for that heritage. In reading the Bible as an adult, though, I often find myself surprised at the ages of various characters because of the way I've seen them depicted over the years. If you have some extra time this week, see what you can discover about the ages of Isaac and his sons Jacob and Esau. What does the text tell us about how old they were when they married, had children, etc.? Record your observations below.

What name did God give him?

What did Jacob ask his wrestling opponent? Did the opponent answer? Who eventually gets the answer to this question?

Did Jacob know who he was wrestling? Explain your answer.

After a night of wrestling Jacob set off to meet his estranged brother, Esau. How did Jacob prepare for this meeting?

How did the meeting go?

Where did Jacob and his clan land?

Digging Deeper

Taking a Dip in the Gospel of Matthew

Rest assured this is not your only opportunity to read Matthew in this course. In *Cookies on the Lower Shelf, Part III* you'll have another opportunity to read all four Gospel accounts. This week, however, if you're running out of material, spend some time in Matthew considering how God's promise to bless the nations through Abraham has ultimate fulfillment in Jesus Christ. Take notes as you go through the genealogy in Matthew 1 and look for significant ties to what we have learned in Genesis.

Week Three: **Same Promise, More Problems**

Genesis 34 tells us about Jacob's daughter, Dinah. Try to remember for future reference the brothers who avenge her with actions that reap lasting consequences. In one case, however, you will see redemption mixed with judgment before the end of Exodus. Keep your eyes opened and watch for it.

Who was Dinah? Who were her full brothers? Who was her mother?

What happened to her?

What did her father Jacob do about the situation?

How did her brothers react?

What happened to Shechem and his people?

What did Levi and Simeon do?

How did Jacob react to their behavior?

After Jacob's two sons kill Hamor and Shechem, God told Jacob to return to Bethel. What was he afraid of?

What did he do before departing for Bethel?

ONE STEP FURTHER:

Genesis 36: The Genealogy of Esau

If you have some extra time, read through Esau's genealogy. The big thing to remember about Esau is repeated throughout this chapter. Esau is the father of the Edomites who live in the land of Edom. Edom is located SOUTHEAST of the Dead Sea. The Edomites, like the people of Aram, are Israel's extended FAMILY.

When Jacob and his clan traveled to Bethel, how did the people in the cities along the way react? Why?

What did God tell Jacob in this chapter? How does it compare with what He said to Abraham and Isaac?

What happened to Rachel along the way to Bethlehem?

Notes

Week Three: **Same Promise, More Problems**

What did Reuben do and what consequence resulted? (The consequence will be revealed later in the text. If you know it, record it. If not, you'll find out soon enough!)

What happened to Isaac? Who makes another appearance on the scene at the close of the chapter?

@THE END OF THE DAY . . .

If Abraham gives hope to the flawed, how much more Jacob, the father of the nation of Israel? Of course, hope does not lie in a flawed person but in a perfect God who has redeemed people like Abraham, Jacob, you, and me (Exodus 15:13; Luke 1:68).

As you finish off your study for the week, take 30 minutes to an hour to meditate on what you have read. Consider the ways God worked through (and in spite of) Abraham, Isaac, and Jacob. Ask Him to put deep in your heart the truth you most need to embrace from the text this week and record it in the space below. Then write down how you will begin to apply this truth in your life.

WEEK FOUR
So You Think *You're* in a Pit?

*But Joseph said to them, "Do not be afraid, for am I in
God's place?"As for you, you meant evil against me, but
God meant it for good in order to bring about this present
result, to preserve many people alive."*
—Genesis 50:19-20

*"Come to Me, all who are weary and heavy-laden,
and I will give you rest."*
—Matthew 11:28

Life is tough. If you're facing hardship and trial right now, you're not alone. It's part of the fundamental reality of living in a fallen world. Sometimes we're not keen on accepting this truth. Often we look the other way and approach life as though it *should* turn out right all of the time, as though problems are the exception rather than the rule. *One day,* we think, *life will be right and I can start living.* One day problems will be gone, that is part of the Christian hope, but it is a future hope. While we sojourn on a fallen earth the trick is learning how to live in this foreign land in a God-honoring way.

As we dive into the story of Joseph this week, lessons abound not only for living but also for thriving while facing life's fastballs, curveballs, and even spitballs. While people often label the Bible as distant and detached from 21st century life, Joseph's life features family favoritism, attempted murder, blended family issues, sexual harassment, false charges of rape, and wrongful imprisonment—and that's just the beginning!

This week let's look for clues from Joseph's life on how to live fully, particularly when life seems to continually be moving from bad to worse.

THIS WEEK:

**Main Reading
14 chapters**
– Genesis 37–41: Joseph's early years

– Genesis 42–45: The hungry brothers

– Genesis 46–50: How Israel landed in Egypt

Additional Reading

**More Reading and
Even More Reading!**
– Catch up on reading you've missed

OR

– Free read wherever you'd like in the Bible.

Following the Story . . .

In the beginning, God created. Adam and Eve fell. Cain killed Abel and Eve gave birth to Seth. Enoch walked with God while the rest of the world sinned. Later Noah showed himself blameless. God saved Noah, his family, and two of every kind of animal from a worldwide flood.

After Noah people chose to build a tower to reach the heavens. This arrogance to "make a name for *themselves*" at the expense of exalting God's name could not thwart God's purposes. At the Tower of Babel He humiliated this arrogance by confusing the people's language and scattering them.

Eventually God called Abram to leave Ur of the Chaldeans. He promised him a land (Canaan) and a seed (Isaac) through whom the Messiah would come. God eventually changed Abram's name to Abraham which means "father of nations." Abraham believed God and it was credited to him as righteousness.

REMEMBERING

Before you start reading this week, take a couple of minutes to summarize the story from last week. Remember, we're going for short, simple, and memorable. Check your notes or Bible only if needed.

READING THE STORY

JOSEPH: the EARLY YEARS
OBSERVE the TEXT of SCRIPTURE

READ about the early years of Joseph in Genesis 37–41. You'll note that there is also a "Meanwhile Back at the Ranch" section about Joseph's brother Judah in Genesis 38.

RECORD a summary of what you learn about Joseph and Judah in this section.

RECORD key words and phrases you noticed.

DISCUSS with your GROUP or PONDER on your own . . .
JOSEPH, the FREE TEEN

Who was Joseph? Briefly describe his family.

Do you notice any repeating familial sins? If so, what?

How can we break patterns of familial sins?

Does favoritism roost in any branches of your family tree? Explain as appropriate. If so, how can you apply truth to correct the situation? Why did Joseph's brothers hate him? Was there more than one reason?

What did they plan to do to him?

ONE STEP FURTHER:

Word Study: Pit
If you have some time this week, find the Hebrew word translated *pit* in Genesis 37 and see where else it appears in Joseph's life. Record your observations below.

COOKIES ON THE
LOWER SHELF™
Putting Bible Reading Within Reach

ONE STEP FURTHER:

Leah's Boys

Jacob's first four sons were born to Leah. Each plays a significant role in the events of Genesis and the descendants of two of them play enormous roles in the history of Israel. Although Leah bore other children later in life, I always remember the first four as a group. If you have some extra time this week, look a little further into the lives of Leah's boys and record your observations below.

Reuben

Simeon

Levi

Judah

What did Reuben suggest and why? Where was Reuben in the birth order?

What role did Judah play in the plan?

Who were the Midianites related to? If you don't remember, where can you look for the answer? What resource can you use?

Are the "Midianites" and "Ishmaelites" in Genesis 37 the same or different people? Explain your thinking. After you've reasoned through this on your own, compare your answers with any you can find in commentaries.

When Joseph finally arrived in Egypt, he was sold to Potiphar. How is Potiphar described? (This is important information. Look closely at the text and record Potiphar's position and ways he's referred to in the text.)

MEANWHILE BACK AT THE RANCH with JUDAH

While the latter part of Genesis clearly follows Joseph, we have a sideroad, a "meanwhile back at the ranch" chapter in Genesis 38 that fills us in on Joseph's brother Judah who "accidentally" sleeps with and impregnates his daughter-in-law. Where on earth do people get the idea the Bible is all about "good guys"?

Who was Tamar? How was she related to Judah?

What did Tamar do and why?

Where does Tamar appear in the New Testament?

JOSEPH: SLAVE, PRISONER, VICE PRESIDENT

What did Joseph do in Potiphar's house?

Describe Joseph's appearance.

How did Joseph respond to "Mrs. Potiphar's" advances?

FYI:

The Scepter
Although Reuben is the firstborn, we're told that the ruler of the people will come from Judah.

The scepter shall not depart from Judah, nor the ruler's staff from between his feet, until Shiloh comes, and to him shall be the obedience of the peoples.
　　　—Genesis 49:10

Jesus, the ultimate ruler, is referred to in Revelation as the Lion from the Tribe of Judah:

. . . and one of the elders said to me, "Stop weeping; behold, the Lion that is from the tribe of Judah, the Root of David, has overcome so as to open the book and its seven seals."
　　　—Revelation 5:5

Week Four: **So You Think You're in a Pit?**

According to the text and based on Potiphar's actions, how did Potiphar view Joseph?

What finally happened between Potiphar's wife and Joseph?

Based on your observation, who or what do you think Potiphar is angry with and why?

Where did Potiphar put Joseph? (As you answer, consider Genesis 39:1, 20 and 40:3.)

Describe Joseph's time in prison.

Who ended up in the same jail as Joseph?

Who put these two new inmates under Joseph's charge? Is it who you would have expected? Why/why not?

What dreams did the two men have?

How did Joseph become involved with the dreams?

What finally happened?

How much time passed between the end of Genesis 40 and the beginning of Genesis 41? Where was Joseph during this time?

What happened to Pharaoh? What service was he looking for?

Who provided Pharaoh with the needed information?

What story did the cupbearer tell? Where, specifically, had he been confined?

Who was the captain of the bodyguard? According to Genesis 40 who had put Joseph in charge of the cupbearer and the baker?

ONE STEP FURTHER:

The Captain of the Bodyguard

Take a little time this week to list everything you learn about the captain of the bodyguard in Genesis.

How did Joseph wind up in front of Pharaoh? What happened when he arrived?

Did Joseph claim any credit? Explain.

What happened to Joseph as a result? How old was he?

What did Joseph name his sons? What does this say about him?

How does your attitude toward trial compare with Joseph's?

What can you learn from his perspective on life? How will you apply it?

READING THE STORY
THE HUNGRY BROTHERS
OBSERVE the TEXT of SCRIPTURE

READ Genesis 42–45 and briefly summarize below.

RECORD key words and phrases you noticed.

DISCUSS with your GROUP or PONDER on your own . . .

While Joseph ruled Egypt, what was his family experiencing back home?

Who went to Egypt to buy food?

Why did Jacob prevent Benjamin from going?

What happened when the brothers arrived in Egypt?

How did the topic of Benjamin come up?

COOKIES ON THE LOWER SHELF™

Putting Bible Reading Within Reach

Week Four: **So You Think You're in a Pit?**

What curveball did Joseph throw at his brothers?

What brothers are mentioned by name in this chapter? Where in the birth order are they? Which mother did they belong to? What did each do according to the narrative?

What surprise did they find on the way home?

How did Jacob react to the news that they cannot buy more food unless Benjamin returns with them?

What was the family situation at the beginning of Genesis 43?

How did Judah help solve the problem?

Was it significant that Judah intervened as opposed to one of the other brothers? Explain.

What did Joseph do when the brothers arrived?

How did Joseph react when he saw his youngest brother?

How did Joseph seat the brothers at dinner?

What happened when the brothers headed for home?

What accusation did Joseph make?

ONE STEP FURTHER:

The Perspectives of Jacob and Joseph

If you have some extra time this week, compare how Jacob and Joseph dealt with hardship and loss. Consider how their losses differed and how this may have affected their outlooks.

Jacob:

Joseph:

What is your biggest takeaway from looking at the perspectives of Jacob and Joseph?

COOKIES ON THE LOWER SHELF™

Putting Bible Reading Within Reach

Notes

ONE STEP FURTHER:

Word Study: Wept
If you have some time this week, look up the Hebrew word translated *wept*. When do we see Joseph weeping? Under what circumstances do we typically see weeping in the Bible? Record your observations below.

Week Four: **So You Think You're in a Pit?**

Where was the cup? Why was its location such a big deal?

What danger was Benjamin in?

How did Judah help?

When did Joseph finally reveal his identity to his brothers?

Describe Joseph's perspective on the events that brought him to Egypt. How did this impact his attitude toward his brothers? Toward God?

What can you apply from Joseph's attitude? How?

What happened to the rest of his family?

What finally convinced Jacob that Joseph was alive?

COOKIES ON THE LOWER SHELF™
Putting Bible Reading Within Reach

READING THE STORY
HOW ISRAEL LANDED IN EGYPT
OBSERVE the TEXT of SCRIPTURE

READ Genesis 46–50 and briefly summarize below.

RECORD key words and phrases you noticed.

DISCUSS with your GROUP or PONDER on your own . . .

What did God tell Jacob?

As you read the genealogies, which names did you recognize? Are you surprised by how many you know?

How many people relocated to Egypt? Who did that number include?

How did Pharaoh respond to Joseph's family?

Week Four: **So You Think You're in a Pit?**

Where did Joseph's family settle? What kind of land was it?

ONE STEP FURTHER:

Older and Younger

The blessing of Ephraim and Manesseh inverts the expected order. If you have some extra time this week, explore other places in Scripture where a younger son ends up with a higher rank than the older. Record your observations below.

How did Jacob describe his life to Pharaoh? (v. 9) How does this compare with Abraham's assessment of his life?

What happened in Egypt as the famine progressed?

How did Joseph's family fare during this time?

How long did Jacob live in Egypt before he died?

What did Jacob say about Ephraim and Manasseh? What did this have to do with the future division of the land?

When Joseph brought the boys to Jacob to bless them, what did he do out of the ordinary?

Does this call to mind anyone else?

Before he died, what did Jacob tell Joseph about the future of their people?

What did Jacob say about his sons? Did he give good words, hard words, or a combination? Explain.

What did Jacob say about Reuben? Do you remember any associated events?

What did he say about Simeon and Levi? What will happen to them? (Keep this in mind as we're going to see massive redemption in upcoming weeks!)

What do we learn about Judah? What long-term ramifications does this have?

Where did Jacob ask to be buried? Ironically, which wife did he end up next to?

COOKIES ON THE
LOWER SHELF™

Putting Bible Reading Within Reach

Week Four: **So You Think You're in a Pit?**

What did Joseph do when Jacob died? Was Pharaoh okay with this? Explain. (Keep this in mind when we come to Exodus.)

What concern did the brothers have? How did Joseph respond to their concerns?

What does this tell us about Joseph's view of God? How does your view of God compare with Joseph's? Do you need to make any adjustments? If so, what kind?

What did Joseph ask the sons of Israel to do when he died?

@THE END OF THE DAY . . .

Joseph lived a roller-coaster life—from favored son to slave to "vice president" of Pharaoh's kingdom. His life was tumultuous but he was strapped in. God held him firm through the ups, downs, twists and turns.

As we close our time this week, spend some time considering where your life feels out of control and remembering the One who holds you firm. You don't have to write anything down, just think and dwell on God's sovereignty over every aspect of your life.

COOKIES ON THE LOWER SHELF™
Putting Bible Reading Within Reach

WEEK FIVE
Delivered from Despondency and Bondage!

"Say, therefore, to the sons of Israel, 'I am the LORD, and I will bring you out from under the burdens of the Egyptians, and I will deliver you from their bondage. I will also redeem you with an outstretched arm and with great judgments. Then I will take you for My people, and I will be your God; and you shall know that I am the LORD your God, who brought you out from under the burdens of the Egyptians.

'I will bring you to the land which I swore to give to Abraham, Isaac, and Jacob, and I will give it to you for a possession; I am the LORD.' "

So Moses spoke thus to the sons of Israel, but they did not listen to Moses on account of their despondency and cruel bondage.
—Exodus 6:6-9

THIS WEEK:

Main Reading
12 chapters
– Exodus 1-12: Out of Egypt

Additional Reading —————

More Reading
1 chapter
– Acts 7

Even More Reading!
7 chapters
– Exodus 25-31: Tabernacle worship

Who hasn't seen Charlton Heston part the Red Sea as Moses in the Academy Award–winning tale of *The Ten Commandments?* The events surrounding Israel's exodus from Egypt were bigger than life as water turned to blood, frogs over-ran an entire country, and food fell from the sky in the wilderness—and these are just the highlights! It's a great read but there's a sense in which Exodus is hard to relate to. After all, when was the last time you dealt with gnats, flies, and locusts of (I can't resist!) biblical proportions?

Consider the people themselves, though. The Israelites didn't listen to the good news Moses brought them because they were hopelessly enslaved. Does that hit a nerve? Know anybody who's lost hope? Know anyone in bondage to debt? Addictions? Expectations? Anything else? Ever feel hopeless yourself?

They also displayed another chronic sin that persists to this days: grumbling. In spite of God's goodness the Israelites grumbled their way through the wilderness because they had to trust God each day for their survival.

COOKIES ON THE LOWER SHELF™
Putting Bible Reading Within Reach

Week Five: **Delivered from Despondency and Bondage!**

Following the Story . . .

God. Creation. Adam and Eve. Cain and Abel. Seth. Enoch. Noah and his kin. Babel. Abraham and Sarah. Isaac and Ishmael.

Isaac married Rebekah who Abraham's servant brought from Padam Aram, the land of his relatives, northeast of Canaan (which becomes Israel). After Rebekah's twenty barren years, Isaac prayed for her and she gave birth to twins Esau and Jacob. Jacob, the second born, opportunistically bought the birthright from his brother and then, at the instruction of his mother, stole the blessing. He fled to the land of Aram where he married his Uncle Laban's daughters, Leah and Rachel.

REMEMBERING

Before you start reading this week, take a couple of minutes to summarize events from last week. Remember, we're going for short, simple, and memorable. Check your notes or Bible if you need to.

READING THE STORY
ENSLAVED in EGYPT
OBSERVE the TEXT of SCRIPTURE

READ Exodus 1–4 to find out what happened when a ruler arose in Egypt who did not know Joseph.

RECORD a summary of the situation and note the main character introduced.

RECORD key words and phrases you noticed.

DISCUSS with your GROUP or PONDER on your own . . .

How many in Joseph's family went to Egypt? Using a concordance, find out where else this has been recorded.

How did the Hebrews fare in Egypt?

What political turn of events took place? How did it affect the children of Israel? What did the Egyptians fear?

What were the midwives told to do? How did they respond? How did God respond to what they did?

Can you think of any modern parallels and applications? Explain.

As Exodus 1 closes, what did Pharaoh command concerning Hebrew baby boys?

ONE STEP FURTHER:

What did Moses float in?

If you have some extra time, do a quick word study on the Hebrew word the NASB translates *basket* in Exodus 2:3. If you've never studied online, these instructions will help you get started.

1. In your computer browser, **type www.blueletterbible.org**

2. Under heading "New Bible Search," **type Exodus 2:3** in search box; **select NASB** from pull down menu under "Version." **Click "Search"** button.

3. You should see six blue boxes to the left of Exodus 2:3. **Click the "C" box.**

4. **Click on the entry "H8392"** located to the right of the word *basket.* This Strong's Concordance number will bring you to every usage of the Hebrew word *tebah (basket)* in the Old Testament.

5. **Read** through the list and **record** what you learn below. Make sure you note who was saved from what, and how God worked in the situation.

Notes

After Moses was born what short-term action did his mother take? Long-term?

FYI:

When did the Levites become *The Levites?*
When Moses was born a Levite (Exodus 2), the tribe had not acquired a good reputation or official status yet. In fact the last value judgment on them was a dying Jacob's saying they would be "dispersed" and "scattered" as a result of the incident with Dinah (Genesis 49:7). Stay tuned!

Before casting Moses adrift on the Nile, what additional steps did Moses' mother take?

Who found Moses? What happened?

FYI:

Another Ark
While Noah was saved in an ark about the size of a football field, Moses was saved in an ark not much bigger than a football.

When Moses grew up, what did he do that changed his life forever?

Where did Moses flee? Who did he meet? What did he do? How long did he stay?

What life-altering event happened when Moses was shepherding his flock?

When did God speak to Moses? What did He say?

How did Moses respond?

Have you ever responded to God this way? Explain.

Did God speak clearly to Moses? Was anything left in question?

As Exodus 4 opens, what did Moses ask?

How had Moses changed after forty years of tending sheep?

What handicap did Moses attempt to excuse himself with? Can you relate to this?

How did God respond to Moses' objections? What application can you make in your life from this account?

Notes

COOKIES ON THE LOWER SHELF™
Putting Bible Reading Within Reach

Week Five: **Delivered from Despondency and Bondage!**

Digging Deeper

Cross-Referencing: Acts 7

Cross-referencing is a key inductive study tool. While scholars continue to write commentaries on the Bible—and many prove very helpful—the best commentary on Scripture remains Scripture itself. If you have time this week, read Acts 7 for Stephen's commentary (recorded by Luke) on the history of his people. Pay close attention to what he says about Moses. Here are a few questions to get you started:

What does Acts 7 tell us about timing in Moses' life?

Does Acts 7 agree with Moses' assessment of his speaking skills? Explain.

What historical gaps does Acts 7 fill in?

What additional questions do you have after comparing the Exodus account with Acts 7?

ONE STEP FURTHER:

Meeting Jethro

What do we know about Jethro? If you have some extra time this week, see what you can discover about Moses' father-in-law from the text and record your findings below.

How did Aaron become involved?

What odd event took place on the way to Egypt? If you're not sure what's going on here, think about going **One Step Further** with the sidebar this week.

How did the Israelites respond to the message Moses and Aaron gave them?

OBSERVE the TEXT of SCRIPTURE

READ Exodus 5–12 and follow Moses' return to Egypt. You can skim the genealogy in 6:14-30—from Jacob's sons to Aaron and Moses.

RECORD a summary of God's actions to free Israel from Egypt.

RECORD key words and phrases you noticed.

COOKIES ON THE LOWER SHELF™

Putting Bible Reading Within Reach

Week Five: **Delivered from Despondency and Bondage!**

DISCUSS with your GROUP or PONDER on your own . . .

How did Pharaoh respond to God's message that Moses and Aaron delivered? What did he say?

How did he retaliate against the Hebrew people?

What did Moses do when the people turned on him?

Have you ever responded this way? How can you improve in the future?

How did God reassure Moses at the beginning of Exodus 6?

According to Exodus 6:9, why didn't the people listen to Moses?

Will slaves to sin react any differently today when we bring God's message to them? How does God break them down? What should we always do first when faced with obstinacy?

The PLAGUES

What will Egypt know when God stretches His hand out against them?

How old were Moses and Aaron? Summarize the major segments of Moses' life to this point.

What can you apply to your life from these major breaks? Are we ever too old for God to use us? If we're currently stuck in a spiritual desert, should we expect to be there the rest of our lives? Explain.

What do Moses' experiences teach about God's mercy and grace after willful rebellion? How can you apply this?

FYI:

Ease of Word Studies in Logos

One of the reasons I use Logos Bible Software is the ease with which I can do a word study. I simply **hover** over the word in question, **right click,** and **drag down** to the Englishman's Concordance entry to run a full search. You can do the same thing with free online tools but it will take you a little longer.

BLOOD   1

Describe the first plague according to Exodus 7. Was it replicated? Explain.

FROGS   2

What option did Moses give Pharaoh when he called for relief from the frogs?

When did Pharaoh ask for frog removal? Do you find this odd? Why/why not?

Digging Deeper

Thinking through the Sovereignty of God

This entire section highlights a difficult theological issue that is reprised in Romans 9: *How can we account for man's responsibility in the context of God's sovereignty?* The Bible teaches both and we must learn to trust that both are true even if we cannot reconcile them in our minds. Is God sovereign? Yes. Is man responsible for his motives, choices, and actions? Yes. Spend some time this week searching the Word for both truths. Reason through your findings in the space below.

After the frogs were gone, how did Pharaoh change?

Have you ever chosen to stay in a "frog" situation instead of seeking God's help? Why?

GNATS   3

What was different about the gnat plague? Why did it matter?

FLIES   4

How was God going to distribute the flies? Why?

When the swarm of flies was announced, what difference was announced with it? Where were the flies? Why?

What did Pharaoh offer Moses while plagued by the flies? How did Moses respond? How did things end up?

LIVESTOCK   5

How was God going to differentiate the livestock of Israel and Egypt?

COOKIES ON THE
LOWER SHELF ™
Putting Bible Reading Within Reach

Week Five: **Delivered from Despondency and Bondage!**

When would this happen? Have you seen this word used before? Where and when?

When Pharaoh confirmed that Israel's livestock was alive, what did he do?

BOILS   6

Describe the next plague. What group was afflicted?

According to verse 14, what does God say the Egyptians will know as a result of the plagues?

HAIL   7

How much advance warning did God give before raining hail on Egypt?
What mercy did He show for those who choose to listen?

Where did the hail *not* fall?

How did Pharaoh respond? What did he do? What did he ask Moses and Aaron to do?

How did Pharaoh change when the threat was removed?

LOCUSTS   8

When God announced locusts, how did Pharaoh's servants respond?

What did Pharaoh suggest this time? How did it go?

What happened to Pharaoh's heart? How does this compare with other references to his heart?

DARKNESS   9

When darkness came over Egypt, what happened in the dwellings of Israel?

What did Pharaoh suggest this time? How did Moses respond?

Are you ever tempted to negotiate God's clear commands? Explain. What did you learn from this account about this?

ONE STEP FURTHER:

Jesus the Lamb of God
If you have some time this week, examine how the Passover lamb points to Jesus, the Lamb of God. Record your findings below.

Notes

ONE STEP FURTHER:

Exodus 25–31
If you have time read about Israel's worship in this section. Record what you learn. Start by considering the following categories:

Sanctuary

Furniture

Other Items

Clothing

DEATH   **10**

What was the final plague? What was its outcome and scope?

What did the Israelites ask their Egyptian neighbors for? Why? What did God do on their behalf?

According to the text, what did the Egyptians think of Moses?

Why didn't Pharaoh let the people go?

Describe the Passover lamb.

What did God command the people of Israel to do with this lamb? Its blood? The leftovers?

According to verse 11, how were they to eat them?

Why did they put blood on their doorposts? What happened to those who didn't?

What were the people to tell their children when they asked about Passover?

Did the people obey God's commands here? What happened?

How did Israel plunder the Egyptians?

@THE END OF THE DAY . . .

We looked at a familiar account this week. As we close out spend some time reviewing Exodus. What truth did you see this week that you haven't noticed before? How will you begin to apply it?

COOKIES ᴼᴺ ᴛʜᴇ
LOWER SHELF™
Putting Bible Reading Within Reach

Week Six: **Delivered from Despondency and Bondage!**

Week Six

A Long Walk with a Difficult People

*Then Moses came and recounted to the people all the
words of the LORD and all the ordinances; and all the
people answered with one voice and said, "All the words
which the LORD has spoken we will do!"*
—Exodus 24:3

Ever taken a car trip with a disgruntled toddler or shared an airplane with a cranky
infant? A long journey is tough enough but a long journey with difficult people always
seems endless.

After spending his first 40 years in a palace and his second 40 years in a desert
tending sheep, Moses spent his last (and, if possible, longest!) 40 years leading
newly freed people with grumbling ingrained in their souls. This week we'll continue
our journey with the people of Israel across the Red Sea and onward toward the
Promised Land, grumbling all the way!

THIS WEEK:

Main Reading
12 chapters
– Exodus 13-20

– Exodus 24: Covenant established

– Exodus 32-34: Golden calf incident;
God declares His name to Moses

Additional Reading ———————

More Reading
3 chapters
– Exodus 21-23: Laws

Even More Reading!
9 chapters
– Exodus 35-40: How to build a
tabernacle

– Hebrews 8-10

– Start reading Leviticus

COOKIES ON THE LOWER SHELF™
Putting Bible Reading Within Reach

Notes

OBSERVE the TEXT of SCRIPTURE

READ the Exodus 13–20 account of God's delivering the children of Israel out of Egypt and starting their journey toward the Promised Land.

RECORD a summary of their early days in the wilderness.

RECORD key words and phrases you noticed.

DISCUSS with your GROUP or PONDER on your own . . .

The EXODUS

Remembering all of Pharaoh's attempts to negotiate favorable terms for himself, how did the final deal go down? Who and what left Egypt with Moses?

What commandments did Moses speak to the people according to Exodus 13?

What promise was imbedded in the commands?

What were the people instructed to tell their sons about their actions?

Do you remember God's actions on your behalf? Your family's? Your church's?

Can you think of ways to remember? Who are some people in your scope of influence? How can you help them remember?

According to Exodus 14:4, who did God say He will be honored through? What else did He say will happen?

How did Israel's attitude change? What caused it?

When the people of Israel were frightened, how did they behave toward Moses? Toward God?

Take a few minutes to consider some application points. What can you learn from the Israelites' fear that is applicable to your leading and to supporting your leaders?

How did Israel escape?

ONE STEP FURTHER:

Word Study: Grumble
Take some time this week to find the Hebrew word translated *grumble*. Where else does it appear in Exodus? In the rest of the Old Testament? What can you learn from Israel's negative example? Record your observations below.

The SONG OF MOSES

Briefly recap the Song of Moses in Genesis 15. What did the people know about God? How had God saved them?

What was Miriam called? Do you know any other biblical women described this way? If not, don't worry; just keep your eyes open!

After the stunning victory over Egypt and the song of joy, what is recorded next?

How did the people react when they drank the bitter water? How should they have responded given God's proven faithfulness?

Do you ever forget God's faithfulness like the Israelites? When you do, how can you remind yourself of His character and ways? Right now, what specific attributes of God and scriptures come to mind?

GRUMBLE, GRUMBLE, TOIL AND TROUBLE

When did the "no water" experience of chapter 15 happen?

When did the grumbling start according to Exodus 16?

What did the people accuse Moses and Aaron of doing? How many were involved?

What did God do for the people?

Who were they really grumbling against?

Do you grumble against God? When are you most tempted to grumble? Why?

Did God meet all of the people's needs? How long did He feed them?

What can we learn from God's faithfulness to Israel?

ONE STEP FURTHER:

Exodus 21–23

Read the laws listed in Exodus 21–23 if you have time this week. What did God command the people to do? What did He command them *not* to do? Record your observations below.

WATER, a FATHER-IN-LAW, a MEAL, and a MOUNTAIN

What was the point of contention in Exodus 17?

What did Moses fear?

How does the quarrel in Exodus 17 compare with the grumble in Exodus 16?

What did God tell Moses to do to get water?

What major character makes his first appearance in Exodus 17?

What happened with Amalek? What did God tell Moses to do?

Who was Jethro? What did we learn about him earlier in the text?

What did Jethro observe in Moses?

How much time was Moses "putting in at the office"?

How did Jethro influence Moses? What did he tell him? How did Moses respond?

What can you learn from Jethro to apply in your life?

Where was Israel camped as Exodus 19 opens? When was this?

What did God tell Moses to tell the people?

How did the people respond (v. 8)?

Week Six: **A Long Walk with a Difficult People**

According to verse 11, what's going to happen?

What restrictions did God make? What consequences?

What happened when the LORD descended on Mount Sinai (v. 18)?

How important was it that the people not break through? How do you know?

What are the ten commandments?

What characterizes the first half of the commandments? The second half?

Do you think any of the commandments are harder than other ones? Why?

OBSERVE the TEXT of SCRIPTURE
The Covenant

READ Exodus 24 and note the covenant God makes with Israel.

RECORD a summary of the main points of the chapter.

RECORD key words and phrases you noticed.

DISCUSS with your GROUP or PONDER on your own . . .

Who is mentioned by name in Exodus 24? Why are they significant?

What did Moses, Aaron and his two sons, and the seventy elders see and experience?

Who else was mentioned by name later in the chapter?

What happens at the end of Exodus 24? How long was Moses on the mountain?

Digging Deeper

Tabernacle Building 101

If you're up for a challenge this week, finish Exodus and learn how to build a tabernacle! Consider how much detail carpenters and artists needed to build this structure precisely, as God commanded.

After you've read the "How To" section in Exodus, compare the text with Hebrews 8–10. It will be well worth investing your time to see the New Testament view. Record your observations and thoughts below.

Exodus 35–40

Hebrews 8–10

OBSERVE the TEXT of SCRIPTURE

The Golden Calf Incident; Moses Sees God

READ Exodus 32–34 and note the contrast between the people of Israel and Moses their leader.

RECORD a summary of the golden calf incident and Moses' interaction with God.

RECORD key words and phrases you noticed.

DISCUSS with your GROUP or PONDER on your own . . .

What did the people do when Moses delayed on the mountain?

How did Aaron handle the situation? How did the people respond?

How did newly freed slaves get gold? (Don't guess; look at the text we just read.)

What did Moses do when he arrived at the camp?

Week Six: **A Long Walk with a Difficult People**

How did God respond?

On what basis did Moses intercede for the people?

What did the Levites do?

At the outset of the Exodus 33, what does God tell Moses to do?

Why?

How did the people take the news?

Describe Moses' relationship with God.

Where did Joshua spend his time?

Why did Moses argue that God should go with them? How did God respond to his request?

What did Moses ask to see?

How did God describe Himself to Moses as He passed by him?

How does this attribute affect you? Don't rush this answer. Think of some specific applications.

What did God command His people concerning the inhabitants they will encounter in the new land? Why?

What else did He command?

How long did Moses remain on the mountain with God?

The book of Exodus closes with these words after the tabernacle is completed.

34   Then the cloud covered the tent of meeting, and the glory of the LORD filled
     the tabernacle.

35   Moses was not able to enter the tent of meeting because the cloud had
     settled on it, and the glory of the LORD filled the tabernacle.

36   Throughout all their journeys whenever the cloud was taken up from over
     the tabernacle, the sons of Israel would set out;

37   but if the cloud was not taken up, then they did not set out until the day
     when it was taken up.

38   For throughout all their journeys, the cloud of the LORD was on the
     tabernacle by day, and there was fire in it by night, in the sight of all the
     house of Israel.

—*Exodus 40:34-38*

@THE END OF THE DAY . . .

So you made it through Exodus! If you didn't finish, that's okay—some is always better than none and we'll make sure to leave some wiggle room for catch-up in future weeks.

As we close this week, spend some quiet time with God asking Him to take what you've learned this past week and cement one or two life-changing truths to your heart.

Remember, growth comes one step at a time and is more often measured in inches than miles. Just keep headed and moving in the right direction!

WEEK SEVEN
Rules, Regs, Serpents and Such

These are the commandments which the LORD commanded Moses for the sons of Israel at Mount Sinai.
—*Leviticus 27:34*

Then the LORD spoke to Moses in the wilderness of Sinai, in the tent of meeting, on the first of the second month, in the second year after they had come out of the land of Egypt, saying, "Take a census of all the congregation of the sons of Israel, by their families, by their fathers' households, according to the number of names, every male, head by head from twenty years old and upward, whoever is able to go out to war in Israel, you and Aaron shall number them by their armies."
—*Numbers 1:1-3*

I often wonder what cash threshold would actually motivate people to read Leviticus and Numbers—two often misjudged books of God's Word. When was the last time you heard anyone talk about these books without a gasp or eye roll?

Our mission this week is two-fold: to see the value of Leviticus and Numbers so we can read and enjoy them and, as always, apply the truths to our lives! You're going to be amazed at the truths we discover!

Notes

Following the Story . . .

God. Creation. Adam and Eve. Cain and Abel. Seth. Enoch. Noah and kin. Babel. Abraham and Sarah. Isaac and Ishmael. Isaac married Rebekah and twenty years later their twins Esau and Jacob were born. Jacob married Leah and Rachel and became the father of the twelve tribes of Israel. Joseph's brothers sold him into slavery but he eventually became "vice president" of Egypt. During a time of great famine, Jacob and the rest of the family relocated to Egypt.

REMEMBERING

Before you start reading this week, take a couple of minutes to summarize the events we studied last week. Short, simple, and memorable. Check your resources if you need them.

READING THE STORY

Leviticus knocks many people off the Bible read-through train. It's a 27-chapter mountain filled with God-given regulations for the children of Israel. It contains everything they needed to know about what offerings to give and when, what was clean and unclean, how to live in accordance with God's laws, as well as the blessings for obedience and the curses for disobedience. Quite honestly, there are some "don'ts" listed in the text so blush-worthy and self-evident it's hard to believe they have to be pointed out! But alas, God included them for a reason.

While most of the book presents rules and regulations, Leviticus 10 recounts a chilling account about Nadab and Abihu, Aaron's two sons who offered strange fire before the LORD. We're going to read this one together.

OBSERVE the TEXT of SCRIPTURE

READ Leviticus 10 taking special note of what Nadab and Abihu did.

RECORD a summary of the situation.

RECORD key words and phrases you noticed.

DISCUSS with your GROUP or PONDER on your own . . .

Who were Nadab and Abihu? What special privileges did they have?

What did they do? What happened after this?

Does anything in the text hint at what may have been the root cause of their actions? Explain your thoughts.

ONE STEP FURTHER:

Leviticus 16: The Day of Atonement

Sitting in the middle of the book of Leviticus is the critical teaching on the Day of Atonement in chapter 16. If you have time this week, read and take note of what happened on this day once every year exactly six months after Passover. Record your observations below.

Digging Deeper

Compare Leviticus and Hebrews

Leviticus gets bad press. There's no other way to put it. When read with a proper mindset, however, Leviticus is an interesting, helpful, and important read. And when it's read in conjunction with the New Testament book of Hebrews—look out!

So if you want to dig this week, read Leviticus comparing it with the letter to the Hebrews as you go. My strong suggestion is to read Leviticus in not more than three sittings, preferably one or two. Pray. Get a mocha. And get into the groove!

Record your findings below. Remember to look for both similarities and differences and for the "better than" statements in Hebrews.

ONE STEP FURTHER:

Leviticus 25: Land Sabbath and Year of Jubilee

The sabbath first appears in Genesis 2. While we typically associate it with people resting from work according to Leviticus 25, God also commanded His people to rest *their land* every seven years. This may seem like an old and isolated rule but it comes into play later in Judah's history when the land rests for 70 years as its people are off it, in captivity (2 Chronicles 36:21). If you have some extra time this week, read Leviticus 25 and take note of what you learn about the sabbath for the land and the Year of Jubilee. Record your observations below.

Digging Deeper

Numbers, Numbers, Numbers

If you're ready to take on another challenge, read (or listen to) the entire book of Numbers this week. You'll note that it starts off a little slowly but picks up speed around chapter 9. Don't get bogged down by what you don't understand at this point. Read, enjoy, and save some discovery for the next time around. As you read, jot down questions and thoughts below.

ONE STEP FURTHER:

Leviticus 26: Blessings and Curses

When the people of Israel entered the Promised Land they took possession, armed with a knowledge of how to live there securely. In Leviticus 26 God clearly told them what to expect if they obeyed or disobeyed. If you have time this week, read through Leviticus 26 and record what you learn about the blessings and curses.

COOKIES ON THE LOWER SHELF™
Putting Bible Reading Within Reach

FYI:

Blessing the Sons of Israel

22 Then the LORD spoke to Moses, saying,

23 "Speak to Aaron and to his sons, saying, 'Thus you shall bless the sons of Israel. You shall say to them:

24 The LORD bless you, and keep you;

25 The LORD make His face shine on you, And be gracious to you;

26 The LORD lift up His countenance on you, And give you peace.'

27 "So they shall invoke My name on the sons of Israel, and I then will bless them."

—Numbers 6:22-27

READING THE STORY

Numbers certainly features a bunch of numbers, but it's also loaded with fabulous accounts that include the ground opening up to swallow people, a donkey who talks, and at least one other story that slides past most Sunday School curricula due to its gore factor.

As Numbers opens, God tasks Moses with taking a census of the people of Israel—numbers, numbers, numbers!! Beginning chapters cover this census, give more information about the priests, Levites, laws and offerings, and recount the Passover celebrated in the wilderness at Sinai. We'll pick up our reading in Numbers 11 after the children leave their camp base at Sinai and go back to their grumbling travels.

OBSERVE the TEXT of SCRIPTURE

READ Numbers 11–14 watching closely how the leaders behave. You may want to mark different types of leaders in order to see their differences clearly.

RECORD a summary of the situation.

RECORD key words and phrases you noticed.

DISCUSS with your GROUP or PONDER on your own . . .

Who complained in this chapter? About what?

What did the people want?

What did Moses ask for?

How did God answer him? Does this sound familiar?

What upset Joshua? How did Moses respond to him?

What was for dinner? Was there enough for seconds?

Have you ever noticed how complaining has a viral affect? How often do you carry and transmit the virus? How can you correct this behavior?

How did Miriam and Aaron get themselves into trouble according to Numbers 12?

What did they say against Moses?

Week Seven: **Rules, Regs, Serpents and Such**

What did Aaron and Miriam think about themselves?

What does Numbers 12:3 tell us about Moses' character?

What did God do? How was the situation resolved?

Is there anything we can learn about respecting God's appointed leaders? Record your thoughts below, citing supporting scriptures. (If you want to address the issue of self-appointed leaders, interact with this topic also. Again, cite a scriptural basis.)

A CRITICAL TURNING POINT: Numbers 13

Where were the people of Israel according to the beginning of Numbers 13?

Who was sent to spy out the land? How are these men described?

FYI:

13

Here's another easy mnemonic device for you. Numbers 13 is where everything starts going south for Israel! No, there's no bad luck, just a bunch of bad choices! Sure makes me think twice!

What information were they looking for? Should the answers have made a difference in how they were going to proceed? Why/why not?

Do you remember what "the Negev" is (v. 22)?

How long were the spies in the Land? This number will become very significant later in the text.

What differing reports did the spies bring?

Which spies urged Israel to take the land and why?

How did the people react to the report?

When did the people of Israel face bad odds before? How did these situations turn out?

ONE STEP FURTHER:

Numbers 18: Duties of the Priests

In Numbers 18 God clearly defines the duties and the responsibilities of priests. If you have some extra time this week, read Numbers 18 to see what God commanded the priests to do and how He took care of them. Record your observations below.

How should their recalling these events have governed their responses now? Did *any* of them learn from God's actions in the past? Explain.

Does knowledge about God and His ways affect your actions in daily life?

Can you improve in this area? How?

What bad decision is recorded in Numbers 14:4?

How did Joshua react?

What did the people decide to do according to Numbers 14:10? Who showed up and what happened?

What did God say He was going to do? How did Moses intervene?

Who gets to enter the land? Who doesn't? Why not?

What was different about Caleb? What can you learn from Caleb's experiences that you can apply to your own?

How long will the people wander? Why this number?

What happened to the ten spies who brought the bad report?

How did the people react to the judgment on the ten?

What happened when they decided to go into the land anyway? Where was Moses?

COOKIES ON THE LOWER SHELF™

Putting Bible Reading Within Reach

Week Seven: **Rules, Regs, Serpents and Such**

What lessons can we learn about obedience (timing, etc.) from this loaded passage?

This section of Numbers moves back and forth between laws and events. The events give helpful context for the rituals (rules and regulations) which may seem harsh when read in isolation. I'm speaking here specifically of the penalties for defiant sin, sometimes referred to as sin "with a high hand," for which no sacrifice is available. We saw this sin in the report of the bad spies, the people's subsequent refusal to enter the land, and then their foolhardy change of mind after God told them it was too late. We'll see another high-handed sin this week as we look at the rebellion of Korah—it's one of the stories I never learned as a kid in Sunday School!

OBSERVE the TEXT of SCRIPTURE

READ the account of Korah and his pals in Numbers 16–17 taking note of both arrogant and humble attitudes you see.

RECORD a summary of the situation.

RECORD key words and phrases you noticed.

DISCUSS with your GROUP or PONDER on your own . . .

Who was Korah?

What did Korah complain about?

How did Moses respond to him?

What did God want to do according to Numbers 16:21? How did Moses and Aaron respond?

What happened to Korah and his rebel friends?

How did the people react on the next day?

What happened then?

In order to quiet some of the grumbling, what did God tell Moses to do?

Week Seven: **Rules, Regs, Serpents and Such**

What did Moses gather from each of the twelve tribes and for what purpose?

Where was Moses told to put Aaron's rod and why? Where else in the Bible is the rod referred to?

What lessons can we learn from Korah's hubris? From Moses' humility?

OBSERVE the TEXT of SCRIPTURE

READ Numbers 20–25 paying careful attention to God's clarity.

RECORD a summary of the events in these chapters.

RECORD key words and phrases you noticed.

DISCUSS with your GROUP or PONDER on your own . . .

Who dies at the beginning of Numbers 20?

In the "wake" of this, what repeated complaint and accusation did the people make?

What did God tell Moses and Aaron to do?

What did Moses do?

FYI:

Don't Mess with Moab
It's ironic that the Moabite king was so set on trying to get Balaam to curse Israel out of fear for Moab's destruction when Scripture records that God told Moses to leave Moab alone. Check out the words of Deuteronomy 2:9: "Then the LORD said to me [Moses], 'Do not harass Moab, nor provoke them to war, for I will not give you any of their land as a possession, because I have given Ar to the sons of Lot as a possession.'"

How did God respond after Moses disobeyed His direct command? Did He provide the water?
What else happened as a result?

What country refused Israel passage? Whose descendents were they?

What happens at the close of Numbers 20? Why was Aaron unable to enter the Promised Land?

What problems recur at the beginning of Numbers 21? What did the people say against God and Moses?

What happened this time?

How did the people respond?

What did God do?

Where does the New Testament speak of this account and with reference to what other event? If you don't know, search "serpent" in a concordance.

Where else is it mentioned in the Old Testament? Again, if you don't know, search on the phrase "bronze serpent" and see what you can find. What significance does this account have?

We see Israel on the move and running into peoples they've had experiences with. How were the people of Israel related to the people of the following nations?

• Edom?

• Moab?

How did Israel try to deal with the Amorites? Did it work?

What happened?

Who else did God give into Israel's hands?

A TALKING DONKEY

Where is Israel at the opening of Numbers 22?

Who was concerned about their location? Why?

Who did the king send for? What did he ask him to do?

What did God tell Balaam?

What did Balaam tell the men from Moab?

ONE STEP FURTHER:

More about Balaam
If you have some time, use your concordance to see what else you can find out about Balaam that sheds light on the events in Numbers 25:18. Record your findings below.

COOKIES ON THE LOWER SHELF™
Putting Bible Reading Within Reach

How did the King of Moab take the answer?

Look closely at Numbers 22:18-19 to see what Balaam told the servants and what he ended up doing.

What did God tell Balaam this time?

What can we learn about God from Numbers 22:22?

What did Balaam's donkey see and do?

What did the angel of the LORD say about Balaam's way (v. 32)?

What did the angel of the LORD clearly tell Balaam according to verse 35?

Where does King Balak take Balaam at the close of Numbers 22?

What do Balaam and Balak do at the opening of Numbers 23?

What word did God put in Balaam's mouth?

How did Balak react?

What did Balak and Balaam try next and what happened?

Did they change their tactics according to Numbers 23:27?

What does Balaam do immediately at the beginning of Numbers 24?

COOKIES ON THE LOWER SHELF™

Putting Bible Reading Within Reach

Week Seven: **Rules, Regs, Serpents and Such**

What did Balak do after Balaam blessed Israel for the third time?

What else did Balaam say before he went home?

How did the Israelites sin against God?

How did God judge them?

Who was Phinehas and what did he do?

How many Israelites died as a result of this sin and God's judgment?

OBSERVE the TEXT of SCRIPTURE

READ Numbers 27 paying special attention to the concerns of women and to the transfer of leadership to Joshua.

RECORD a summary of the events in this chapter.

RECORD key words and phrases you noticed.

DISCUSS with your GROUP or PONDER on your own . . .

What did Zelophehad's daughters ask Moses for?

What did Moses do?

What was God's verdict?

What does God tell Moses he will see?

Why did God not let Moses enter the Promised Land?

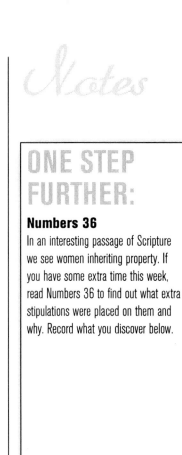

ONE STEP FURTHER:

Numbers 36
In an interesting passage of Scripture we see women inheriting property. If you have some extra time this week, read Numbers 36 to find out what extra stipulations were placed on them and why. Record what you discover below.

COOKIES ON THE LOWER SHELF™

Putting Bible Reading Within Reach

Week Seven: **Rules, Regs, Serpents and Such**

What did Moses pray?

Who replaced Moses? Who gave him the position?

What did God tell him to do for Joshua?

OBSERVE the TEXT of SCRIPTURE

READ Numbers 31 to find out what happens to Midian and why.

RECORD a summary of the events in this chapter.

RECORD key words and phrases you noticed.

DISCUSS with your GROUP or PONDER on your own . . .

What did God tell Moses to do before being "gathered to [his] people"?

How many men did Moses send after the Midianites?

What were God's people avenging?

Why do you think Phinehas was sent out to lead? Where had he proven himself?

Why was Balaam killed? What role had he played?

How thorough was the destruction of Midian? Why?

OBSERVE the TEXT of SCRIPTURE

READ Numbers 32 focusing attention on what happened on the other side of the Jordan River.

RECORD a summary of the events in this chapter.

RECORD key words and phrases you noticed.

DISCUSS with your GROUP or PONDER on your own . . .

Why did Reuben and Gad want to stay in the land of Gilead on the east side of the Jordan River?

Putting Bible Reading Within Reach

Why was Moses concerned about Reuben and Gad's request?

How did Reuben and Gad's men respond?

What happened?

How long were the fighting men of Reuben, Gad, and the half-tribe of Manasseh to remain with Israel?

@THE END OF THE DAY . . .

Wow! If you read all the material this week you read a ton—and even if you just stuck with the main text, you probably waded into a lot of uncharted territory! Congratulations on a job well done! As we close this week, record any changes in how you view Leviticus and Numbers.

Take some time to be quiet before God to consider the most significant truth He taught you this week. Record your thoughts below.

WEEK EIGHT
The Catch-Up Episode!

These are the words which Moses spoke to all Israel
across the Jordan . . .
—Deuteronomy 1:1a

Although Moses was one hundred and twenty years old
when he died, his eye was not dim, nor his vigor abated. So
the sons of Israel wept for Moses in the plains of Moab . . .
Since that time no prophet has risen in Israel like Moses,
whom the LORD knew face to face.
—Deuteronomy 34:7-8a, 10

We're inclined to credit television writers with inventing the catch-up episode, but God's sovereignty is always light-years ahead! So if you missed the first giving of the Law in Exodus, if you missed the wilderness wanderings or battles in Numbers, Deuteronomy will help you catch up. If you're solid on these books Deuteronomy will help you review. While Deuteronomy is filled with more rules and regulations, you'll see that even here following God is a matter of the heart!

THIS WEEK:

Main Reading
19 chapters
– Deuteronomy 1-11

– Deuteronomy 27-34

Additional Reading

More Reading
15 chapters
– Deuteronomy 12-26

Even More Reading!
– You pick. Catch up if you need to or simply meditate on the Words that you've been reading over the past several weeks.

Notes

Week Eight: **The Catch-Up Episode!**

Following the Story . . .

God. Creation. Adam and Eve. Cain and Abel. Seth. Enoch. Noah and his kin. Babel. Abraham and Sarah. Isaac and Ishmael.

Isaac married Rebekah. Twenty years later Rebekah gave birth to their twins, Esau and Jacob. Jacob married Leah and Rachel and became the father of the twelve tribes of Israel. Joseph's brothers sold him into Egyptian slavery but God eventually raised him up to become "vice president" of Egypt. During an enormous famine, Jacob and the rest of his family relocated to Egypt. Eventually a new Egyptian ruler assumed power. Not "knowing" Joseph, he enslaved the Hebrews for 400 years. But God raised up Moses to deliver this small clan that had multiplied over those years to become a great nation.

REMEMBERING

Before you start reading this week, take a couple of minutes to summarize the history we read about last week. Short, simple, and memorable. Check your resources if you need them.

READING THE STORY
OBSERVE the TEXT of SCRIPTURE

READ Deuteronomy 1–4.

RECORD a summary of this section.

RECORD key words and phrases you noticed.

DISCUSS with your GROUP or PONDER on your own . . .

Where are the children of Israel at the beginning of Deuteronomy? Who is speaking?

FYI:

Where we're at . . .

Deuteronomy takes place in the land of Moab across the Jordan River from Jericho. It is also referred to as the "Transjordan" region.

COOKIES ON THE LOWER SHELF™

Putting Bible Reading Within Reach

When did this take place?

How did God respond to Moses when he was overwhelmed with the burden of leadership?

According to the Deuteronomy text, whose idea was it to send spies into the land?

What event did Moses call the people to remember (Deuteronomy 1:30)?

What did the people do instead? What happened to them?

How can we benefit by recalling God's favor to us? What can you recall and how will this impact your thinking about the future?

Once they were shut out of the Promised Land, what did Israel do?

Week Eight: **The Catch-Up Episode!**

Although Israel wandered for forty years due to disobedience, how well did God care for His people? Explain.

When were the children of Israel given another shot at the Promised Land?

Who did God command Israel not to harass? Why?

What happened when Israel encountered Edom and Moab?

What happened with King Sihon? What nation did he rule?

Why did Israel succeed? What can we learn from this for today?

How many of King Og's cities did Israel defeat?

What kind of cities did Israel conquer according to Deuteronomy 3:5? Why is this significant?

Describe the extent of their conquests.

What tribes did Moses give this land to? Thinking back to your previous reading, how did this part of Israel's inheritance differ from the rest? What conditions applied to the inheritance?

What did Moses tell Joshua to do? Who was fighting for Israel?

Why is the LORD angry with Moses at the end of Deuteronomy 3?

According to Deuteronomy 3:28 what was Moses to do for Joshua? What can we learn about leading from this?

ONE STEP FURTHER:

Dealing with Fearful People

In Deuteronomy 2:4-5a, the following statement is made in regard to the Edomites: ". . . they will be afraid of you. So be very careful, do not provoke them . . . ." Consider how fearful people are easily provoked. How can we deal wisely with people in this emotional state? Support your answer.

COOKIES ON THE LOWER SHELF™

Putting Bible Reading Within Reach

Notes

Week Eight: **The Catch-Up Episode!**

How can you improve the leader skills of those who will follow you?

ONE STEP FURTHER:

Edomites

Take some time to see what else you can learn about the Edomites. Use all your resources then show where Edom lies in relation to Israel on your map. Record your findings below.

What does Moses command the people at the beginning of Deuteronomy 4?

What danger lay in forgetting?

What did Moses tell them to remember?

How can we apply exhortations to remember (not forget) today? Record some ideas below.

What was Israel to guard against?

How is Israel described in Deuteronomy 4:20?

What does "a people of God's own possession" mean? How do we live in light of this truth?

FYI:

Sihon and Og . . . Batting Practice
The defeats of Sihon and Og—two Amorite kings from beyond the Jordan River to the east—mark the beginning of the conquest of the Promised Land. While their kingdoms lay outside Canaan's borders to the east, they both messed with Israel and served as something of a warm-up, batting practice if you will, as Israel approached the Jordan River and Jericho beyond. The people of Jericho remembered what God did in Egypt and their hearts melted with fear when they heard about Sihon and Og's downfall.

What will happen to the people if they don't obey?

What does God promise the nation if they seek Him from the place of their captivity?

How does Moses describe God in Deuteronomy 4?

According to Deuteronomy 4:40, what will happen if Israel obeys God?

OBSERVE the TEXT of SCRIPTURE

READ Deuteronomy 5–11.

RECORD a summary of the section.

RECORD key words and phrases you noticed.

COOKIES ON THE LOWER SHELF™
Putting Bible Reading Within Reach

Week Eight: **The Catch-Up Episode!**

DISCUSS with your GROUP or PONDER on your own . . .

Which of the ten commandments do you think our culture most rails against? Explain.

What characterizes the first half of the commandments?

How about the second half?

How did the people react to God's glory?

How does Deuteronomy 5 close?

Why did Moses give these commandments? Who were they directed toward?

What is the command in Deuteronomy 6:4?

What did God want Israel's relationship to Him to be characterized by?

How were they told to teach their children? How can you obey this commandment today?

FYI:

Shema

Deuteronomy 6 contains what Jewish people refer to as the Shema. Shema is the Hebrew word for "Hear." You see this beginning in verse 4: "Hear, O Israel! The LORD is our God, the LORD is one!" God calls His people to love Him with their whole heart, remember Him, and diligently teach their children all day every day so they too will remember and obey.

What benefits will Israel soon receive? Did they work for them? Will they get them?

What temptation did Moses warn them to guard against?

What similar temptations do we face today? How can we guard against them?

When will the people likely forget God? Can we, under this condition? Explain.

How does Israel compare with the nations it dispossessed?

FYI:

A Couple of Rules

When God gives a command there is always a reason. Sometimes He reveals a reason. For example, according to Deuteronomy 7 God commanded Israel *not* to make covenants with the people of the land they were entering; rather, they were told to utterly destroy them. God also told them *not* to intermarry with these peoples. He warned that intermarriages will eventually turn their hearts from Him. (Read the story of Solomon lately?) Again we see that obedience is both right and beneficial.

ONE STEP FURTHER:

How Solomon Fell

Check out Solomon's life to see how his disregard for God's commandments led to his eventual downfall.

Week Eight: **The Catch-Up Episode!**

Why did Israel win?

What did God tell them to do when they won?

TWO MAJOR RULES

What two actions are prohibited in Deuteronomy 7? Why?

What did God tell the people to do with idols they encountered?

Why did God choose Israel according to Deuteronomy 7:7-8?

What did He promise Israel if they obeyed?

What did he tell the people to remember when they became afraid?

Why shouldn't God's people dread their enemies?

Will God wipe out Israel's enemies all at once? Why/why not?

According to Deuteronomy 8:1, why does God command His people to be careful to obey His laws?

What did God do to the people in the wilderness? What was the lesson?

What practical miracles did He do for them?

What kind of land was God bringing them into?

What does Deuteronomy 8:11 warn about?

FYI:

God Tends the Land of Israel

Deuteronomy 11:10 tells us the land of Israel is different from the land of Egypt. There's no Nile River running through it; it gets its rain from God: "a land for which the LORD your God cares: the eyes of the LORD your God are always on it . . . ." (v. 12). According to verses 13-14, rain comes with obedience. It's interesting how rain dependency and God dependency are integrated. As Jesus said, "Seek first the kingdom and all [the things you need] will be added to you."

Week Eight: **The Catch-Up Episode!**

What sin is linked with forgetting? Is this relevant to our daily lives? How can we be more careful to remember?

Again, how did Israel stack up against the nations it was going to dispossess? (Not the first time it's been said!) What specifics about some of the people are given here?

Who will win the battle for Israel? Explain.

Why did God drive the other nations out? Did it have anything to do with Israel being righteous? Explain.

How is Israel described in Deuteronomy 9:6?

What was one behavior that characterized them?

COOKIES ON THE LOWER SHELF™

Putting Bible Reading Within Reach

According to Deuteronomy 9:14, what did God want to do to Israel?

What event did Moses recall and retell in Deuteronomy 9:15ff.?

How long did Moses fast before the LORD on behalf of the people? What was the outcome?

What did he recall and retell in Deuteronomy 9:23?

What characterized the people of Israel? Are we any different?

In spite of the people's shortcomings, how did Moses describe them in Deuteronomy 9:29?

What does Moses recount at the beginning of Deuteronomy 10?

COOKIES ON THE
LOWER SHELF™
Putting Bible Reading Within Reach

Notes

Week Eight: **The Catch-Up Episode!**

According to Deuteronomy 10:12, what does God require? How can you apply this in your life this week?

According to Deuteronomy 11:8-9, why did God command obedience?

How will God reward obedience?

How will God punish disobedience?

What are some of the ways Israel was to remember?

Digging Deeper

Digging in Deuteronomy

You can dig deeper this week by reading the rest of Deuteronomy and asking yourself multiple *Who, What, When, Where, Why,* and *How* questions. Then address these questions below: *What role does the heart play in obedience to God's law? Does God want more than external compliance?*

FYI:

Bittersweet Words

Deuteronomy 29–32 marks a bittersweet segment of the book. The days of Moses were ending and Joshua would soon lead. Moses left them with some harsh words: they would fall away, yet God would eventually redeem.

OBSERVE the TEXT of SCRIPTURE

READ Deuteronomy 27–34.

RECORD a summary of the section.

RECORD key words and phrases you noticed.

DISCUSS with your GROUP or PONDER on your own . . .

THE BLESSINGS AND THE CURSES

Deuteronomy 27–28 is important to grasp. The blessings and curses pronounced on Mount Gerizim and Mount Ebal describe what Israel will respectively reap for obedience or disobedience. Understanding the prophets hangs on these chapters so grab a cup of coffee and let's focus in.

What did Moses tell Israel to do with the stones when they crossed over the Jordan?

What else did he tell them to build?

Who did Moses command to stand on Mount Gerizim to bless the people? Do you notice a common denominator in the group?

What group was commanded to stand on Mount Ebal?

What breaches of covenant were called out?

What kind of offense did most of the curses address?

What did the people have to do for the blessings?

What blessings did God promise?

How many times is "if" used in 28:1-13? How is it used?

What will happen if they disobey? List some specifics.

FYI:

The Song of Moses
The Song of Moses told what will happen when Israel rebels in the future. It served as a witness against the people when their rebellion came to pass.

COOKIES ON THE
LOWER SHELF™
Putting Bible Reading Within Reach

REVIEWING THE PAST, LOOKING TO THE FUTURE

Describe the covenant with Moab. Was it a second one or a renewal of the one made at Horeb? Explain.

Who did Moses address? According to Deuteronomy 29:10-11, who specifically did he include?

What was the message? What facts and events did Moses recount?

What miracles did the people of God witness? What was God's purpose for these miracles?

How adept are you at remembering God's works in both biblical history and your personal life? Can you point to a recent example of God showing His faithfulness to you? If not, ask Him to remind you since we, like the Israelites, can be quick to forget. Record your thoughts below.

According to Deuteronomy 30, what does Moses say Israel will remember and do in lands they're scattered to?

What will God do? How many times and ways does He say this?

What will God do for His people and their descendants?

What will happen to Israel and her enemies?

What choice is set before Israel as Deuteronomy 30 closes? What outcomes are attached to each?

PASSING THE BATON

How old is Moses now? Do you recall the mention of his age at other significant points? If so, divide his life into three major segments and describe each one.

Who did Moses focus on as the people's deliverer?

What did he say to Joshua?

Week Eight: **The Catch-Up Episode!**

How often was the Law supposed to be read to the whole assembly, including women, children, and foreigners living within Israel? Why?

What did God tell Moses about the future of Israel?

According to Deuteronomy 31:20, when will Israel's problems start? How can we apply this to our lives?

What was the purpose of the song?

Where were the people supposed to keep the book of the Law?

How is God described in this poem referred to as The Song of Moses? What specifics do we learn about Him?

How did God protect and nurture Israel according to the lyrics?

How are the people described? How was their behavior a direct affront to God?

What did God do about it?

What is Moses told at the end of the chapter?

What lessons have you learned so far from Israel's disobedience?

MOSES' BLESSINGS ON EACH SON OF ISRAEL

When did Moses speak these blessings?

What did he say about each son?

Which son did he omit?

Week Eight: **The Catch-Up Episode!**

How did Moses' blessing to Levi differ from what Jacob said?

How were Jacob's words to Levi fulfilled, specifically with regard to land?

How did Joseph's blessing differ from his brothers'?

Who's the focus in the final verses? How does this affect Israel?

Where did Moses die?

Who buried him?

What did Moses get to see before he died? How specific is the description?

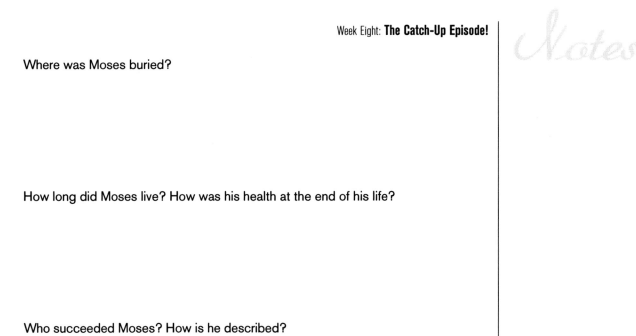

Where was Moses buried?

How long did Moses live? How was his health at the end of his life?

Who succeeded Moses? How is he described?

What final words about Moses are spoken in Deuteronomy?

@THE END OF THE DAY . . .

Genesis. Exodus. Leviticus. Numbers. Deuteronomy. We've made it through the Torah, the Pentateuch, the books of Moses! In *Cookies on the Lower Shelf, Part III* we'll see how important Jesus thought these books were—but that is a study for another day. Spend some time today thanking God for His Word and His faithfulness. Ask Him to impress on you the truth you most need to focus on from His Word at this time in your life. Don't rush this. Take a walk, power down the electronics and spend some time in God's presence listening. Then jot down what He brings to mind.

Notes

Week Eight: **The Catch-Up Episode!**

WEEK NINE
The Secret to Victorious Living

"Only be strong and very courageous; be careful to do according to all the law which Moses My servant commanded you; do not turn from it to the right or to the left, so that you may have success wherever you go.
—Joshua 1:7

Victory—we're all looking for it one way or another. Not everyone has the "competitive gene" (as we call it in my family!) pushing them to win at everything from baseball to verbal repartee, but who doesn't want a life of victory? Joshua is a book of victory! In its pages we see lives lived in obedience to God and His Word and the good results for both individuals and communities. This book of obedience woos us to ask hardcore application questions: *What if I live a life of obedience to God's Word? Can my life be characterized by victory as well? What has to change to order my life according to God's Word?*

The reading load is less than usual this week so slow down, linger in the text and relish these powerful, life-giving words! Ask God to empower you to walk in obedience through the power of His Spirit! Enjoy!

THIS WEEK:

Main Reading
12 chapters
– Joshua 1-9
– Joshua 22-24

Additional Reading ————

More Reading
5 chapters
– Joshua 10-12
– Joshua 13-14

Even More Reading!
7 chapters
– Joshua 15-21

MEMORIZE:

Be strong and courageous!
"Have I not commanded you? Be strong and courageous! Do not tremble or be dismayed, for the LORD your God is with you wherever you go."
—Joshua 1:9

COOKIES ON THE LOWER SHELF™
Putting Bible Reading Within Reach

Following the Story . . .

God. Creation. Adam and Eve. Cain and Abel. Seth. Enoch. Noah and his kin. Babel. Abraham and Sarah. Isaac and Ishmael. Isaac and Rebekah. Jacob and the twelve tribes. Joseph. Egypt. Enslavement. Exodus. Wilderness. See, the more you know it, the less it takes to prompt your recall!

REMEMBERING

Before you start reading this week, take a couple of minutes to summarize events in the book of Deuteronomy.

JOSHUA

The first half of the book of Joshua moves along at a nice clip as God's people enter and begin taking possession of the Promised Land under Joshua, Moses' successor. As you read, you'll want to watch for interesting comparisons within the book and with other books. Since we're reading a smaller amount this week, consider taking some extra time to mark key words and, to borrow a phrase from John Piper, to "respectfully ransack the text." The second half of the book deals with dividing the land and doling it out to the twelve tribes. Those who have the time and inclination will cover this in a **Digging Deeper** section. While the second half of Joshua isn't as easy to read as the first, the precision and order with which the land is apportioned—to say nothing of the very real and historical boundaries—make it very important to read and understand.

READING THE STORY
OBSERVE the TEXT of SCRIPTURE

READ Joshua 1 taking note of God's instructions to Joshua.

RECORD a summary of this chapter.

RECORD key words and phrases you noticed.

DISCUSS with your GROUP or PONDER on your own . . .

What is Israel's situation at the beginning of the book of Joshua? Who was leading? Where were they? How had things changed?

What did God tell Joshua to do? How many times did He repeat His command?

How would Joshua be able to obey God's command?

How can we apply these words today?

What was different about the Reubenites, the Gadites, and the half-tribe of Manasseh?

ONE STEP FURTHER:

Asking Hard Questions
We've talked about it before and we'll talk about it again. Take some time alone with God to consider what changes need to take place for you to meditate on His Word day and night. This is a great excuse to go for a long quiet walk. Record your thoughts below.

Describe the people's attitude in Joshua 1. Were their hearts inclined toward obedience or disobedience? Explain.

What do the people say to Joshua at the end of Joshua 1? Where have we heard these words before?

FYI:

Marking the Text

Marking is an inductive study tool that makes key words jump off the page. Some people resist **marking** texts as unhelpful busy-work. Actually **it** helps key words (and their pronouns) stand out on the page so you can more easily see main points and overall flow. You don't have to **mark** the text to be a good student of the Word but **it** is a powerful tool in the inductive tool box. Any guesses on the key word in this paragraph?

ONE STEP AHEAD:

Marking Rahab

If you have some extra time this week, try your hand at marking Rahab (including pronouns) in Joshua 2.

OBSERVE the TEXT of SCRIPTURE

READ Joshua 2 paying close attention to the woman named Rahab.

RECORD a summary of this chapter.

RECORD key words and phrases you noticed.

DISCUSS with your GROUP or PONDER on your own . . .

What does Joshua do at the start of the second chapter? Did this remind you of anything from Joshua's past? If so, what?

Where did the spies end up?

Describe Rahab from the text.

According to Rahab, what did the people of Jericho know about Israel and how were they responding to their approach?

What did Rahab know about God and what did she do about it?

Who did Rahab save and how?

ONE STEP FURTHER:

Watch for Contrasts

One principle of inductive study is watching for contrasts. In Romans 8, for instance, we see a clear contrast between the flesh and the Spirit. While it's important to watch for contrasts within verses and chapters, we need to realize that there are more global ones. An example of this is the characters of Rahab and Achan. If you have some time this week, compare their lives and actions. Who were they? What did they do? How did their actions impact those around them? Record your observations below.

COOKIES ON THE
LOWER SHELF™
Putting Bible Reading Within Reach

Week Nine: **The Secret to Victorious Living**

Digging Deeper

A God Who Seeks the Nations

Rahab is an example of a non-Israelite, a woman from "the nations," who was grafted in to the people of God in the Old Testament. Spend some time this week digging for other examples of God bringing other people into relationship with Himself.

ONE STEP FURTHER:

What is your river?
Is there a river God is asking you to step into by faith? Something He is calling you to do, but you have no idea how it can work because the water is high and you can't swim? Don't miss these two facts: at the Red Sea God rolled back the water before asking the people to move but at the entry to the Promised Land the priests had to walk into the water and wait for God to stop it *upstream!* Spend some time considering this contrast today and record your response to the question below.

OBSERVE the TEXT of SCRIPTURE

READ Joshua 3–5 and consider the similarities and differences between this water crossing into the Promised Land and the crossing of the Red Sea as the people left Egypt at the beginning of their journey.

RECORD a summary of this section.

RECORD key words and phrases you noticed.

DISCUSS with your GROUP or PONDER on your own . . .

How does this water miracle differ from the one at the Red Sea?

How is it similar?

How did the people prepare themselves?

According to Joshua 3:4, what were the people told to follow and at what distance? Why?

Week Nine: **The Secret to Victorious Living**

What role did the ark play in this drying up of the waters? Explain.

ONE STEP FURTHER:

Dangerous Obedience
Circumcising a nation camped so close to its enemies is dangerous. How are you at obeying when there are risks? Reflect in the space below.

What did God say He was going to do to Joshua? Why?

What did God command Joshua to do with the stones according to Joshua 4? What was their purpose?

FYI:

Stones of Remembrance
Throughout the Bible God tells His people to remember. In Joshua He gives them a specific way to go about it by taking stones from the middle of the Jordan River.

I still have a stone that one of my classmates gave me when we studied Precept Upon Precept Joshua together. It's a reminder that sometimes in life we need to step in the river before God stops the water. One of the questions we talked about in that class was this: *What would you do if you knew God would not let you fail?* The rock is a reminder to me of that class and what we learned together.

I have other "rocks" in my life, too. One is an old computer that I used to write my first book. When I retired that computer I printed out some significant verses and attached them to the computer to help me always remember why I do what I do and Who called me to do it.

Where did he tell them to take the stones from? How often is the phrase repeated?

Do you have any stones of remembrance in your life? How can you incorporate tangible reminders of God's faithfulness into your family tradition?

What did Reuben, Gad, and the half-tribe of Manasseh do according to this chapter? Why was this important?

What question will the people's children ask? How are they told to answer?

COOKIES ON THE LOWER SHELF™
Putting Bible Reading Within Reach

How can you plan to answer questions your children will have about God? Be specific.

What had the people of the land heard about the LORD? How did this affect them?

Why did Joshua circumcise the men?

Where was Israel camped when he did this? In what city (on which side of the Jordan)?

What made the location significant?

What did the people eat while at Gilgal?

Who does Joshua meet at the end of the fifth chapter? What happened?

COOKIES ON THE LOWER SHELF™

Putting Bible Reading Within Reach

FYI:

Judah's Heroes and Villains

One strategy that helps me keep track of characters in the Old Testament is remembering the tribe they're from. It's interesting to note the tribes of both heroes and villains.

While Joshua himself descended from Joseph's son Ephraim, the tribe of Judah stands out in this book with a major hero, a major villain, and a heroine grafted in. Both the faithful spy Caleb and the notorious thief Achan hailed from Judah. Rahab, who recognized Israel's God as the one true God, married into the family!

OBSERVE the TEXT of SCRIPTURE

READ the accounts of the battles at Jericho and Ai in Joshua 6–8. Watch contrasts carefully as you read.

RECORD a summary of this section.

RECORD key words and phrases you noticed.

DISCUSS with your GROUP or PONDER on your own . . .

Why was Jericho shut up so tightly?

What did God command Israel to do to defeat Jericho? How long did it take?

What special instructions did God give the people regarding the goods inside the city? What term describes everything in the city?

How would God punish the disobedient?

What did God command Israel to do to the inhabitants? Why? What did you learn about the inhabitants?

What happened to Rahab? Who did her obedience affect?

After the tremendous victory at Jericho, what awaited Israel at Ai and why?

ONE STEP FURTHER:

Word Study: Under the Ban
The phrase *under the ban* occurs seven times in Joshua 6–7 but the Hebrew word *herem* occurs twelve times in that stretch. What does *under the ban* mean? Is there anything in your life that is under the ban—any sin keeping you from standing firm and living a faithful life?

Who gave Joshua the battle plan for Ai? How did this differ from what happened at Jericho?

How did Joshua respond to defeat? In what way did his response sound like the people? In what way did it sound like Moses?

Why did they lose according to God?

Do you think Joshua could have averted this disaster? Explain your answer.

Week Nine: **The Secret to Victorious Living**

How far did the negative consequences of Achan's sin reach?

Joshua 10–12
When the Israelites entered the Promised Land, fighting began in the southern part of Canaan and moved north. If you have some extra time this week read Joshua 10–12 and follow the action on a map. Record highlights from these chapters below.

Have you ever considered the reach of your own sin? Who else has experienced bad consequences from your actions?

Have you ever experienced consequences from someone else's sin? Explain.

Joshua 13–14
Joshua 13 marks the beginning of land distribution. While it's not the most exhilarating reading, it's still important. Joshua 13 covers the land given to Reuben, Gad, and the half-tribe of Manasseh on the east side of the Jordan River. Joshua 14 opens with faithful Caleb of the tribe of Judah receiving his inheritance. If you have time this week, read these chapters and note your observations below.

What happened the second time at Ai?

How did this battle differ from the one at Jericho? Explain the specifics.

What did Joshua do after the victory at Ai?

Digging Deeper

The Effects of Sin

It's an offensive topic to raise but sin is a big offense. Where else in the Bible do we see the consequences of the sin of one person or a group of people affecting others, even those not personally culpable?

What effects of sin have we seen in Joshua?

What warnings against sin does God give the people?

Think through the books we've read so far. How has sin reached out and affected others?

Genesis

Exodus

Leviticus

Numbers

Deuteronomy

Notes

FYI:

More About the Gibeonites

Like Rahab, the Gibeonites figured out which side they needed to be on when God came to town. While they deceived Joshua to get on his team, there is no evidence that they ever enticed Israel to sin. As far as we know they were never a problem to Israel after they entered into covenant with them.

Saul ended up in deep trouble for messing with them but the Gibeonites did not harm the nation. They are another example of God saving people who humble themselves before Him. In Rahab we saw one person and family; now we see an entire people.

Whom will you serve?

"If it is disagreeable in your sight to serve the LORD, choose for yourselves today whom you will serve: whether the gods which your fathers served which were beyond the River, or the gods of the Amorites in whose land you are living; but as for me and my house, we will serve the LORD."

—Joshua 24:15

OBSERVE the TEXT of SCRIPTURE

READ about the Gibeonite's deception in Joshua 9.

RECORD a summary of this chapter.

RECORD key words and phrases you noticed.

DISCUSS with your GROUP or PONDER on your own . . .

Who were the Gibeonites? Why did they deceive Israel?

What did they know about Israel's God? Did their response to the knowledge of God sound like anyone else's we read about? Explain.

How did the Gibeonite's response differ from the other nations'?

What did they want from Israel?

What was their lie and how did they sell it?

What critical mistake did Israelite leaders make before covenanting with them?

Do we have any indication that this was a repeated mistake? Explain.

How did the situation resolve?

Digging Deeper

Divvying up the Land

If you're up for it, read Joshua 15–21 to find out who got what in the Promised Land. Envision yourself in the land to enjoy its geography and imagine the events we've been covering. Remember, God chose this land to reveal Himself to His special people. Go into as much or as little detail as you want all the while remembering that geography, like many other things in life, is picked up bit by bit over time. Celebrate your new discoveries and realize what you don't know yet is a treasure to find on another day!

OBSERVE the TEXT of SCRIPTURE

READ Joshua 22–24 noting what you learn about the tribes on both sides of the Jordan River. Also pay close attention to Joshua's exit speech.

RECORD a summary of this section.

RECORD key words and phrases you noticed.

DISCUSS with your GROUP or PONDER on your own . . .

What tribes did Joshua address in Joshua 22? Where were they located?

What was the point of contention?

How did the tribes west of the Jordan respond?

Who was sent to assess the situation?

Week Nine: **The Secret to Victorious Living**

Based on the arguments put forth, what had the Israelites learned from some of their past mistakes?

What do you think of their approach to resolving conflict?

Did you learn anything you can apply to resolve conflicts in your life?

As Joshua addressed the people in Joshua 23, what did he attribute Israel's success in battle to?

What did God instruct Israel to do in the days ahead? What verbs does Joshua use?

Considering what God called Israel to do to drive out nations, how can we apply these same words to our lives today? What verbs are usually associated with our pursuit of God and His ways?

If the people associate with the nations, what will happen to them?

When you've "associated" with sin, what has God done to put you back on track?

In Joshua 24 God provides another CliffsNotes summary of history up to the present. What high points does He cover?

Why the reminder here?

What did Joshua call the people to do? What warnings did he give?

Where did this take place? What do you remember about this location? (If you don't remember, don't sweat it!)

According to Joshua 24:31, how long did Israel serve the LORD?

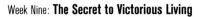
Week Nine: **The Secret to Victorious Living**

@THE END OF THE DAY . . .

Joshua is a book of tremendous victory. Although there are smatterings of defeat sprinkled here and there, we see the people of Israel largely obedient as they complete the journey they began in Egypt. As we close out our study this week, spend some time reviewing what you learned and ask God to cement in your heart the single most important truth for you to learn now from this book. Record it below with some ideas about how you can more fully incorporate it into your everyday life.

WEEK TEN
How Not to Live

In those days there was no king in Israel; everyone did what was right in his own eyes.
—Judges 21:25

Joshua is to Judges as victory is to defeat. While Joshua pulses with victory as Israel enters and begins to possess the Promised Land, Judges resembles a slowly dying man. It's characterized by defeat that comes from people taking their eyes off God. Time and time again they're given into their enemies' hands.

If Joshua is a book about "Do!" Judges is about "Don't!" We can learn from right examples, certainly, but 3-D results and punishments of sin stick with us in compelling ways. While we'll see some examples of obedience early on in the book, the downward spiritual and moral spiral is shocking even by Old Testament standards.

As you try to make heads or tails of crazy thinking and actions, keep in mind the final verse of the book that appears above: "In those days there was no king in Israel; everyone did what was right in his own eyes."

As you jump into this book, measure the people's thinking and behavior against truth and see where it comes up lacking! Not a bad habit to apply to our own thinking and behavior, too, huh?

THIS WEEK:

Main Reading
25 chapters
– Judges 1-5
– Judges 6-9
– Judges 10-12
– Judges 13-16
– Judges 17-21
– Ruth

Additional Reading

Why no "More Reading"?
Judges is jam packed with personal histories. If life throws you a curve, you can skip a section or two of the above readings but you will miss some interesting accounts. Since this is our last week of study, you can use remaining readings to help keep you on course until your next Bible study begins.

Even More Reading!
– Do catch-up reading you need or want.

MEMORIZE:

A Summary of the Time of the Judges
"In those days there was no king in Israel; everyone did what was right in his own eyes."

—Judges 21:25

Week Ten: **How Not to Live**

Following the Story . . .

God. Creation. Adam and Eve. Cain and Abel. Seth. Enoch. Noah and kin. Babel. Abraham and Sarah. Isaac and Ishmael. Isaac and Rebekah. Jacob and the twelve tribes. Joseph. Egypt. Enslavement. Exodus. Wilderness. Jordan River. Gilgal. Jericho. Possession of the land.

REMEMBERING

Before you start reading this week, take a couple of minutes to summarize high points from the book of Joshua.

READING THE STORY
OBSERVE the TEXT of SCRIPTURE

READ Judges 1–5 marking the telling phrase *did not drive out.*

RECORD a summary of this section.

RECORD key words and phrases you noticed. There are several, so have fun!

DISCUSS with your GROUP or PONDER on your own . . .

Looking primarily at the first three chapters, what happened to the people of Israel after Joshua died? How did they live and why?

What summary information in Judges 2 describes cycles that occurred during this time period?

Who judged Israel prior to Deborah?

How did a judge get the job? What did he or she do? How did Israel benefit?

What was Israel's situation during Deborah's time?

What great advantage did Israel's enemies have?

What message from God did Deborah deliver to Barak? How did Barak respond?

What did other women do according to this account? Who delivered the death blow to Israel's enemy?

COOKIES ON THE
LOWER SHELF™
Putting Bible Reading Within Reach

Digging Deeper

. . . there arose another generation after them who did not know the LORD . . .

If you have extra time this week, consider both how quickly and why the people fell away after the deaths of Joshua and the elders who survived him. See what else you can find in the Word about people falling away from God's truth and, based on the text of Scripture, offer your suggestions as to how we can keep from repeating this in generations that follow us.

Notes

FYI:

The Least of the Tribe of Manasseh

Gideon: "O Lord, how shall I deliver Israel? Behold, my family is the least in Manasseh, and I am the youngest in my father's house."

If Gideon had known the full story of his ancestors, he would have known that God sometimes picked the youngest, the least, the unexpected to work wonders!

OBSERVE the TEXT of SCRIPTURE

READ about Gideon in Judges 6–9. Watch the shift in his estimation of himself.

RECORD a summary of this section.

RECORD key words and phrases you noticed.

DISCUSS with your GROUP or PONDER on your own . . .

What was Gideon doing as Judges 6 opens? How did Gideon's situation compare to that of Israel as a whole?

Who was oppressing Israel? What were they doing?

What was significant about where Gideon was threshing?

Why was the angel of the LORD's greeting so ironic?

COOKIES ON THE
LOWER SHELF™
Putting Bible Reading Within Reach

What did the angel of the LORD tell Gideon to do? What assurance did he give Gideon?

ONE STEP FURTHER:

Is putting out a fleece appropriate today?

If you have some extra time this week, reason through this question considering both the context of Judges as well as the impact of the Holy Spirit on our thinking and decision making. Record your observations and conclusions below.

How did Gideon obey?

How are you at obeying when you are afraid? How can you improve in this area? What truths can you bring to mind to help you during these times?

After Gideon took the hard (although covert) stand among his people, who did God send him to deal with next?

How many men did Gideon have available to fight? How did this compare with the numbers of Midianites who consistently invaded Israel?

Why did God eventually whittle the number down to only 300? What truth did the Israelites need to learn?

How can you apply this truth in your life?

In Judges 8 how do you see Gideon changing? How did he deal with the people of Succoth and Penuel? Was his behavior appropriate? Explain your reasoning from the text.

What position did the people want Gideon to assume according to Judges 8:22? How did he respond?

How do you characterize the ending of Gideon's story?

Who was Abimelech? How does his life connect to Gideon's?

What's different about the way Abimelech came to power? How does he differ from Israelite leaders before him?

Are you ever tempted to live Abimelech-style? If so, how does the text correct this thinking?

What can we learn from the company Abimelech kept?

FYI:

Empty Men in the Land of Good

Judges 11:3 tells us Jephthah lived in the land of Tob, which is the Hebrew root for *good*. Don't miss the irony that while he was in "good" land, worthless/empty *(reyq)* men gathered themselves to him.

Digging Deeper

Gideon: Is everything as it appears?

When the people of Israel asked Gideon to rule over them, he seemed to give a godly answer and decline. If you have some extra time, find his show-me-the-money comment and the meaning of the name he gives to his concubine's son. See if your opinion changes.

Here are a few questions to get you started.

What did Gideon ask the people for after his victory?

What did Gideon name his son? What does the name mean?

How did Gideon treat the people?

ONE STEP FURTHER:

Why are they fighting over the land?

If you don't remember the background to this squabble, review Numbers 21:21-31. Israel had held this territory since seizing it on their way to the Promised Land. Record significant observations below.

OBSERVE the TEXT of SCRIPTURE

READ Judges 10–12.

RECORD a summary of this section.

RECORD key words and phrases you noticed.

DISCUSS with your GROUP or PONDER on your own . . .

How does Judges 11:1 describe Jephthah? Does this remind you of anyone else? If so, compare how the same description is used differently.

What region was Jephthah from? What city? On what side of the Jordan River?

How did Jephthah become a judge? How does this compare with the ascendancies of other rulers we've seen in the book of Judges?

What kind of people did Jephthah hang out with? Who else ran in similar circles?

Week Ten: **How Not to Live**

Was God with Jephthah when he fought the Ammonites? How do you know?

What vow did Jephthah make?

We need to closely examine how Jephthah fulfilled his vow to God. Based on the context of Judges 11:30-40, what do you think Jephthah "did" (v. 39) to his daughter and why? List all your reasons.

How long did Jephthah judge Israel? Who followed him?

OBSERVE the TEXT of SCRIPTURE

READ about the life and times of Samson in Judges 13–16.

RECORD a summary of this section.

RECORD key words and phrases you noticed.

COOKIES ON THE
LOWER SHELF™
Putting Bible Reading Within Reach

DISCUSS with your GROUP or PONDER on your own . . .

What tribe was Samson from? What portion of the land was Samson's tribe supposed to possess? Keep this fact in mind since we'll be referring to it in the next section.

According to Judges 13, what were Samson's parents like? What kind of people were they?

Did their actions remind you of anyone else in the book of Judges? If so, who?

What human emotions/desires drove Samson? Cite examples from the text.

How did God use Samson in spite of himself?

Week Ten: **How Not to Live**

OBSERVE the TEXT of SCRIPTURE

NOTE: As we approach the final chapters of the book of Judges, keep in the front of your mind that people are doing what is right in their own eyes. Remember the revealed Word of God as you read these final accounts and hold the actions up to the plumbline of truth.

READ Judges 17–21 keeping in mind what we've just talked about.

RECORD a summary of this section.

RECORD key words and phrases you noticed.

DISCUSS with your GROUP or PONDER on your own . . .

List as many facts as you can from Judges 17. Let me get you started:

> Micah lived in Ephraim.
>
> Micah told his mother he stole her 1,100 pieces of silver.
>
> Micah's mother asked the LORD to bless her son.

Now go back through your list and make a shorter list of the entries exhibiting behavior contrary to the Word of God. Again, I'll get you started:

Micah stole money from his mom.

Mom dedicated the money to make an idol.

If you're in an overachiever mood, cite scriptural references that call these sins.

What "looks right" to those doing what is right in their own eyes? Again, I'll start us off:

Micah did tell mom he took the money.

Mom did want God to bless her son.

Mom dedicated money to the LORD.

Week Ten: **How Not to Live**

As we move on to Judges 18, what political situation are we reminded of?

Why didn't the tribe of Dan have their inheritance?

As you read Judges 18 watch for rationalizations people made for their behaviors. Then list the places where people either wandered or bolted from the Word of God.

Note carefully how Judges 18 closes. How long did idolatry pervade the land? What finally ended it?

Just when we think the situation in the land can't get any worse, another chapter opens reminding us that there is no king in Israel and introducing another problematic Levite. Where did the Levite reside? Where did Micah reside? What tribe was Joshua from?

What happened when the Levite brought his concubine home?

When the Levite and his concubine were en route to Ephraim where did they lodge and why?

How did the decision to stop in this particular city turn out?

Does the city remind you of any other city you've read about? If so, which one? What similarity did you see?

What actions showed the Levite's character? List as many as you can from the text.

How did Israel decide to punish Gibeah? Is there any indication they sought God's counsel?

What caused the escalation with the entire tribe of Benjamin?

When did Israel finally seek God's counsel? What did He say?

What subsequent problem arose in Judges 21?

Notes

How did they solve this? Was God involved?

How does life today compare to life during the time of the judges of Israel? What have you learned that you can apply today?

OBSERVE the TEXT of SCRIPTURE

READ and enjoy the book of Ruth.

Remember that God always has a remnant. Even during the corrupt time of the judges, some people remembered God and followed His ways!

RECORD your observations and thoughts in the space below.

COOKIES ON THE
LOWER SHELF™
Putting Bible Reading Within Reach

@THE END OF THE DAY . . .

Take a quiet walk or sit down with a cup of coffee and spend some time reflecting back over what you have learned since the beginning of our study together. Ask God to impress one or two key truths on your heart to focus on. Ask Him where He would like your attention to be fixed at this specific time in your life. Record your thoughts below.

Here's the biggie as we finish this session of Bible study: *How will you walk with God until Bible study starts up again?* Ask God to put some ideas in your head and then record some possibilities below.

I look forward to seeing you in 1 Samuel for *Cookies on the Lower Shelf, Part II!*

COOKIES ON THE
LOWER SHELF™
Putting Bible Reading Within Reach

RESOURCES

Helpful Study Tools

Arthur, Kay
The New How to Study Your Bible
Eugene, Oregon: Harvest House
Publishers

The New Inductive Study Bible
Eugene, Oregon: Harvest House
Publishers

Logos Bible Software
Available at www.logos.com.

Greek Word Study Tools

Kittel, G., Friedrich, G., & Bromiley,
G.W.
*Theological Dictionary of the New
Testament, Abridged* (also known as
Little Kittel)
Grand Rapids, Michigan: W.B.
Eerdmans Publishing Company

Zodhiates, Spiros
*The Complete Word Study Dictionary:
New Testament*
Chattanooga, Tennessee: AMG
Publishers

Hebrew Word Study Tools

Harris, R.L., Archer, G.L., & Walker,
B.K.
*Theological Wordbook of the Old
Testament* (also known as TWOT)
Chicago, Illinois: Moody Press

Zodhiates, Spiros
*The Complete Word Study Dictionary:
Old Testament*
Chattanooga, Tennessee: AMG
Publishers

General Word Study Tools

Vine, W.E.
*Vine's Complete Expository Dictionary
of Old and New Testament Words*
Nashville, Tennessee: Thomas Nelson

Strong, James
*The New Strong's Exhaustive
Concordance of the Bible*
Nashville, Tennessee: Thomas Nelson

Recommended Commentary Sets

Expositor's Bible Commentary
Grand Rapids, Michigan: Zondervan

NIV Application Commentary
Grand Rapids, Michigan: Zondervan

The New American Commentary
Nashville, Tennessee: Broadman and
Holman Publishers

One-Volume Biblical Commentary

Carson, D.A.
*New Bible Commentary: 21st Century
Edition* (4th ed.). Leicester, England;
Downers Grove, IL: Inter-Varsity Press

COOKIES ON THE
LOWER SHELF™
Putting Bible Reading Within Reach

HOW TO DO AN ONLINE WORD STUDY

For use with www.blueletterbible.org

1. Type in Bible verse. Change the version to NASB. Click the "Search" button.

2. When you arrive at the next screen, you will see six lettered boxes to the left of your verse.

   Click the "C" button to take you to the concordance link.

3. Click on the Strong's number which is the link to the original word in Greek or Hebrew.

Clicking this number will bring up another screen that will give you a brief definition of the word as well as list every occurrence of the Greek word in the New Testament or Hebrew word in the Old Testament. Before running to the dictionary definition, scan places where this word is used in Scripture and examine the general contexts where it is used.

ABOUT PRECEPT

Precept Ministries International was raised up by God for the sole purpose of establishing people in God's Word to produce reverence for Him. It serves as an arm of the church without respect to denomination. God has enabled Precept to reach across denominational lines without compromising the truths of His inerrant Word. We believe every word of the Bible was inspired and given to man as all that is necessary for him to become mature and thoroughly equipped for every good work of life. This ministry does not seek to impose its doctrines on others, but rather to direct people to the Master Himself, who leads and guides by His Spirit into all truth through a systematic study of His Word. The ministry produces a variety of Bible studies and holds conferences and intensive Training Workshops designed to establish attendees in the Word through Inductive Bible Study.

Jack Arthur and his wife, Kay, founded Precept Ministries in 1970. Kay and the ministry staff of writers produce **Precept Upon Precept** studies, **In & Out** studies, **Lord** series studies, the **New Inductive Study Series** studies, **40-Minute** studies, and **Discover 4 Yourself Inductive Bible Studies for Kids**. From years of diligent study and teaching experience, Kay and the staff have developed these unique, inductive courses that are now used in nearly 185 countries and 70 languages.

MOBILIZING

We are mobilizing believers who "rightly handle the Word of God" and want to use their spiritual gifts and skills to reach 10 million more people with Inductive Bible Study by 2015. If you share our passion for establishing people in God's Word, we invite you to find out more. Visit **www.precept.org/Mobilize** for more detailed information.

ANSWERING THE CALL

Now that you've studied and prayerfully considered the scriptures, is there something new for you to believe or do, or did it move you to make a change in your life? It's one of the many amazing and supernatural results of being in His life-changing Word–God speaks to us.

At Precept Ministries International, we believe that we have heard God speak about our part in the Great Commission. He has told us in His Word to make disciples by teaching people how to study His Word. We plan to reach 10 million more people with Inductive Bible Study by 2015.

If you share our passion for establishing people in God's Word, we invite you to join us! Will you prayerfully consider giving monthly to the ministry? We've done the math and estimate that for every $2 you give, we can reach one person with life-changing Inductive Bible Study. If you give online at **www.precept.org/ATC**, we save on administrative costs so that your dollars go farther. And if you give monthly as an online recurring gift, fewer dollars go into administrative costs and more go toward ministry.

Please pray about how the Lord might lead you to answer the call.

PURCHASE WITH PURPOSE

When you buy books, studies, videos and audios, please purchase from Precept Ministries through our online store (**http://store.precept.org/**). We realize you may find some of these materials at a lower price through for-profit retailers, but when you buy through us, the proceeds support the work that we do to:

- Develop new Inductive Bible studies
- Translate more studies into other languages
- Support efforts in nearly 185 countries
- Reach millions daily through radio and television
- Train pastors and Bible Study Leaders around the world
- Develop inductive studies for children to start their journey with God
- Equip people of all ages with Bible Study skills that transform lives

When you buy from Precept, you help to **establish people in God's Word!**

Putting Bible Reading Within Reach